How do you make a Stegosaurus chili?
Take it to the North Pole.

How do we know dinosaurus were ugly?
They never won any beauty pageants.

What is a popular Tyrannosaurus toothpaste?
Dinodent!

Kevin Borden

Also by Alice Saurus
Published by Ballantine Books:

1001 DINOSAUR JOKES FOR KIDS

1001 MORE DINOSAUR JOKES FOR KIDS

Alice Saurus

BALLANTINE BOOKS • NEW YORK

Copyright © 1994 by Dora Wood

All rights reserved under International and Pan-American Copyright Conventions. Published in the United States of America by Ballantine Books, a division of Random House, Inc., New York, and simultaneously in Canada by Random House of Canada Limited, Toronto.

Library of Congress Catalog Card Number: 93-90523

ISBN 0-345-38497-0

Printed in Canada

First Edition: January 1994

Introduction

Can you stand it? Here are another 1,001 hilarious jokes about dinosaurs. Some of them are stories, some of them are riddles, some of them are knock-knocks. They're all funny.

My friends tell me dinosaur jokes all the time. I'm sure if you tell your friends dinosaur jokes that they'll have dino jokes to tell you, too. If you know some dinosaur jokes that aren't in this book, send them to me, and I'll use them in a new book. If you're the first person to send me a joke I haven't already used, I'll give you credit. Write me:

Alice Saurus
P.O. Box 30373
New York, NY 10011

Thanks!

Contents

1001 MORE DINOSAUR JOKES FOR KIDS

A Gnawful Predicament

How do you make Stegosaurus chili?
Take it to the North Pole.

How did Gus the Goofasaurus feel about his new job as a chimney sweep?
It sooted him fine.

What would you get if you crossed a skunk and a Pterodactyl?
Something that stunk to high heaven.

Why did the Triceratops cry when it lost the checkers game?
It was a saur loser.

If a dinosaur died while serving in the army, what would they put on his coffin?
A lid.

Why did the one-handed dinosaur cross the road?
To get to the second-hand shop.

Why did Gus the Goofasaurus blow up the china shop?
He wanted to seeing flying saucers.

What would you get if you crossed a Tyrannosaurus and a mute owl?
A dinosaur that would eat you and not give a hoot about it.

What did the Tyrannosaurus's left big toe say to her right big toe?
"Don't look now, but there are a couple of heels following us."

Why did the Triceratops take off his gloves?
He didn't feel well.

What do you feed a Tyrannosaurus that thinks she's a cat?
Mice Crispies.

2

What is the difference between inflation and a dinosaur's dinner?
One goes up, the other goes down.

What's the difference between Ms. Tyrannosaurus and a postage stamp?
One's a female and the other a mail fee.

What do you call a Tyrannosaurus that steals pigs?
A hamburglar.

Why was the Tyrannosaurus angry with his dinner?
It didn't agree with him.

What happened to the dinosaur that was raised in a small teepee?
He grew to a point.

What time is it when there's a Tyrannosaurus at your front door?
Time to go out the back door.

What did the Tyrannosaurus say when he saw the igloo full of Eskimos?
"Oh, boy, frozen pies!"

Did you hear about the dinosaur etiquette expert?
She knew about manners when Emily Post was a stump.

Why did the Tyrannosaurus put on perfume?
She wanted to hunt for dinner at Bloomingdale's.

Why did the Tyrannosaurus spit out Ronald McDonald?
She didn't like his sesame-seed buns.

What do they call the dinosaur emissary to the United Nations?
The Ambassador-that's-Large.

Why was the Tyrannosaurus so excited when it clouded up?
She was hoping it would rain cats and dogs.

MILLER: That check you gave me for exterminating dinosaurs came back.
BARNEY: So did the dinosaurs.

What happened after the Tyrannosaurus ate the automobile full of people?
She got car sick.

What do they call the surgeon who tried to perform a tonsillectomy on the Carnosaurus?
Lefty.

If you call a dinosaur from Ontario a Toronto-saur, what do you call one from Cuba?
Comrade.

Why did the Tyrannosaurus buy a case of lettuce?
Because he thought he was getting a great deal at twenty-five cents a head.

Why wasn't Larry frightened when the Tyrannosaurus started to chase him?
Because his deodorant promised complete protection.

What do you get if you cross an Ultrasaurus with someone sneaky?
A big creep.

What do you have for dinner when a Tyrannosaurus Rex cooks poultry?
Chicken à la king.

MANDY: I heard your kitty was attacked by your neighbor's dinosaur, Curiosity.
PATTY: Yes, Curiosity killed the cat.

AL: I heard you were telling everybody I was as mean as a Tyrannosaurus and twice as ugly.
DAN: That's not true. I never said you were mean.

What happened to the cook who was eaten by the Tyrannosaurus?
He was deranged.

What happened to the artist's model who was also eaten?
She was deposed.

To the electrician?
He was delighted.

To the horseback rider?
She was dismounted.

To the piano tuner?
He was unstrung.

To the musicians?
They were disbanded.

To the cashier?
She was distilled.

To the secretary?
He was defiled.

To the medium?
She was dispirited.

7

There's never a frightening moment when you're being chased by a Velociraptor. The fear lasts for the rest of your life.

Why did Gus the Goofasaurus put a stick of dynamite in his nostril?
Because he wanted to blow his nose.

What did the Tyrannosaurus say after she caught a knight?
"I hate having to peel these things."

What four things kept the Brontosaurus from being a ballet dancer?
Her feet.

What would you get if you crossed a kitty with a Brontosaurus?
A saur puss.

What do you get if you cross a mink with a Tyrannosaurus?
A fur coat that bites.

What do you get if you cross a Brontosaurus with a bee?
Squashed flowers.

What do you get if you cross a rabbit and a Stegosaurus?
A dinosaur that multiples very quickly.

What do you get if you cross a Triceratops with peanut butter?
A dinosaur that sticks to the roof of your mouth.

What kind of motorcycles do Tyrannosauruses like?
Choppers.

Why did the Pterodactyl fly to the top of the World Trade Center?
The elevator wasn't working.

Why was the Tyrannosaurus limping?
He put his foot in his mouth.

Why did the Tyrannosaurus try to catch the Good Year blimp?
He thought it was a football.

Why did the Tyrannosaurus steal a cannonball?
He wanted to go bowling.

What did the Tyrannosaurus do with the Washington Monument?
He used it for a toothpick.

Did Tennessee Williams write about dinosaurs?
Sure, in *Night of the Iguanadon*.

Was Barbra Streisand ever in a movie about dinosaurs?
Yep. *A Saur is Born*.

What about Judy Garland?
Haven't you seen *The Lizard of Oz*?

Who won the Academy Award for Best Performance by a Dino?
Susan Saurandon.

Was there a dinosaur on the "Mary Tyler Moore Show"?
You bet. Sauris Leachman.

Did one have a role on "M*A*S*H"?
Certainly. Alan Aldasaurus.

Books about dinosaurs:

Dental Care for Your Tyrannosaurus
by Minnie Teeth

Training Your Dinosaur to Polka
by Ivan Knack

How I Lost Twenty Tons: A Diet for Dinosaurs
by Aida Little

Breeding Dinosaurs for Profit
by Ahmed Millions

Milking Dinosaurs
by Kareem Rizes and Phyllis Buckett

Exploring Dinosaur Dens
by Hugo Furst

Selling Footwear to Brontosaurus
by Wendy Shufits

11

Twenty Years as a Dinosaur Tamer
by Maya Storrie

Are Dinosaurs Really Extinct?
by Arthur Enymoore

Interior Decorating for Allosaurus
by Chester Drawers

How to Escape from Any Dinosaur
by Justin Tyme

What looks like a dinosaur and flies?
A flying dinosaur.

What would you get if you crossed a potato
with a Brontosaurus?
Instant mashed potatoes, or a dino that
was all eyes.

How do you know a dinosaur is from Scot-
land?
He's playing the bagpipes.

Why did Chumley run away from the Scottish Tyrannosaurus?
Because it was playing the bagpipes.

What happened to the Tyrannosaurus when the Scottish people heard him playing the bagpipes?
He was kilt.

How could you recognize an Irish dinosaurus?
It was only a wee little thing.

Why were the wee Irish dinosaurs the first ones to be extinct?
Because they kept getting stepped on.

What kind of dinosaur was green and had bumps?
A Pickleosaurus.

Why did the Carnosaurus run away from the chimpanzee?
She thought she was a banana.

Why don't dinosaurs like to talk to goats?
Because they always butt in.

What time is it when a Titanosaurus breaks down your wall?
Time to get a new wall!

Where should you go for a new wall after a Titanosaurus breaks it down?
To Wal-Mart, of course.

Did you hear about the absent-minded dinosaur freak?
He's so crazy about them that sometimes he even forgets. . . .

What do you get if you cross a dinosaur with a chicken leg?
Beats me, but Colonel Sanders would have a hard time dipping it in batter.

What kind of dinosaur goes, "Ha, ha, ha, ha, splat!"
One that's laughing its head off.

What happened when the Tyrannosaurus burst into the Catholic church during services?
Mass hysteria.

14

Why did Penny call her dinosaur Bill?
Because he came to her house on the first of the month.

Why did the Carnosaurus eat the decorator?
Because he had good taste.

Why did George buy oats for his dinosaur?
Because it ate like a horse.

Why did Alicia put her rowdy Triceratops in a stall in the barn?
She wanted to stabilize it.

How can you call a Tyrannosaurus a light eater?
Because as soon as it's light it starts to eat.

Did you hear about the Dryosaurus named Max who wouldn't go mountain-climbing?
They call him Anti-climb Max.

What did Gus the Goofasaurus name his
pet rodent?
Mousey Tung.

What did he name his collie?
Flower.

How about his boxer?
Shorts.

Did he have a pigeon?
Sure, it was named Toad.

A rabbit?
Transit.

Why did Gus decide he wanted to be an
orthopedist?
Because they get all the breaks.

Why did Gus get all bundled up to paint his house?
Because it said on the can to be sure to put on three coats.

Why did Gus buy a paperweight?
He wanted to keep his bills down.

How do we know that Gus's mother was forgetful?
He was already three years old when she laid his egg.

Why was the Pterodactyl spinning in circles?
Because he heard that the whirlybird catches the worm.

How do you hit a Brontosaurus on the nose when it misbehaves?
Stand on a chair.

What happened when Alicia put up a "Beware of Tyrannosaurus" sign on her gate?
Her Tyrannosaurus ate it.

17

Why didn't Alicia have any problems with burglars after she got her Tyrannosaurus? It cost so much to feed it there was nothing left in her house for burglars to steal.

What happened when Gus the Goofasaur got amnesia?
His IQ went up.

Why did Christie call her Tyrannosaurus Camera?
Because it was always snapping.

What's brown and dangerous?
Tyrannosaurus-infested chocolate pudding.

Did you hear about the dinosaur that took a math test?
He passed with extinction.

What note do you get if an Ultrasaurus playing the violin falls down a mine shaft?
A flat minor.

Why did the dinosaur go to bed?
Because the bed wouldn't come to her.

Why did dinosaurs carry umbrellas?
Because umbrellas can't walk.

Have you heard the story about the slippery Brontosaurus?
You wouldn't grasp it.

How did Gus the Goofasaurus get a job as a puppeteer?
He pulled a few strings.

Did you hear that Gus put on a one-man show in the park?
It was so bad that after fifteen minutes four trees walked out.

What happened when Gus ran away with the circus?
The police made him bring it back.

How does a dinosaur get out of a tree?
He waits for fall and floats down on a leaf.

How does a dinosaur get up a tree?
He stands on an acorn and waits.

Why do dinosaurs paint their feet brown?
So they can hide in chocolate pudding.

What do you get if a Titanosaurus steps on Batman and Robin?
Flatman and Ribbon.

Did you hear about the nearsighted Tyrannosaurus that sat down to gnaw a bone?
When it got up it was missing a leg.

Where was the Tyrannosaurus's temple?
On his head.

Why did Gus the Goofasaur close the refrigerator when he saw the mayonnaise?
Because it was dressing.

Where does a Brontosaurus go when it loses its tail?
To a retail outlet.

What happened when Gus built a car with a wooden engine?
It wooden go.

Why did Helen give her Tyrannosaurus a quarter for being good?
Because she didn't want him to be good-for-nothing.

Why did Gus steal the manhole cover?
He wanted to listen to it on his CD player.

Why did Gus give up tap dancing?
He kept falling into the sink.

Why is it noisy when dinosaurs play tennis?
They have to raise such a huge racket.

What did Gus's right eye say to his left?
"Something's come between us that smells."

What's the difference between a Pterodactyl with one wing and one with two wings?
A difference of a pinion.

Why did Gus rip all the bathtubs out of his mansion after he won the lottery?
He wanted to be filthy rich.

Why did Gus buy a book about electricity?
He wanted some light reading.

What should you do if your dinosaur has ticks?
Don't wind him.

22

Why did Gus the Goofasaurus go to sleep under an old car?
So he would wake up oily in the morning.

Did Gus lose weight when he went on a diet of bananas and coconuts?
No, but he sure could climb trees afterward.

What did Gus think of his trip on a flying carpet?
It was rugged.

Why did Gus try to swallow an umbrella?
He wanted to put something away for a rainy day.

How do we know dinosaurs were ugly?
They never won any beauty pageants.

Why did everyone laugh when Gus the Goofasaurus sat down to play the piano?
Because there was no stool.

Why did Gus sit in front of a fan with a BB gun?
He wanted to shoot the breeze.

Why did he want to get his typewriter fixed?
Because the "o" was upside down.

Why was the crossed-eyed man a failure when he opened a dinosaur obedience school?
He had no control over his pupils.

Did you hear about the Tyrannosaurus that grilled a psychic?
He ate her medium.

Why did Gus try to open a bank account with wooden nickels?
He wanted to start a shavings account.

How was the blind dinosaur cured when he became a carpenter?
He picked up a hammer and saw.

How was the mute dinosaur cured by fixing the bicycle?
He picked up the wheel and spoke.

What happened when Gus didn't pay the exorcist?
He got repossessed.

Why did Gus sell his bird dog?
It couldn't fly.

Why didn't Gus peel the orange before he ate it?
He knew what was inside.

Why was Gus hurt after he put a muffler on?
Someone started the car.

Which dinosaurs had eyes?
The ones who owned freezers.

What happens if you drink red wine with dinosaurs?
They get tipsy.

How did the dinosaurs pick their banner?
They took a flag poll.

What do you call a Goofasaurus with half a brain?
Gifted.

What do you call a Tyrannosaurus who practices birth control?
A humanitarian.

What did Gus the Goofasaurus do when no one would sing with him?
He bought a duet-yourself kit.

Did you hear that Gus nearly got one hundred on his history test?
It wasn't ninety-eight, though. It was just two zeros.

Can you get a job looking out for dinosaurs at the North Pole?
Yes, but you have to have good ice sight.

Why did Gus stay after school?
He was trying to figure out where the words went after the teacher rubbed them off the blackboard.

Why did Gus buy a giraffe?
So he could have someone to look up to.

How did Mother Goofasaurus grow so strong?
From raising dumbbells.

Why was Gus afraid of Santa?
He had Claus-traphobia.

Did you hear that Gus overcame his fear of Santa? He even got a job as a Santa at Macy's, but he was fired.
He didn't have the St. Nick knack.

27

What happened when Gus became a marshmallow salesman?
He learned the art of the soft sell.

Who did the bachelor Stegosaurus invite to his party?
Only the Miss Stegs.

What happened to the dinosaur that discovered fire?
He became flamous.

Why did Gus's sister Gertie buy two rubber trees?
She wanted a pair of stretch plants.

What kind of correspondence did Gus send to his senator?
He sent her Capitol letters.

Why did Gus buy a clothes hamper?
He wanted to throw in the towel.

What happened when the Tyrannosaurus ate the frog?
He felt hoppy.

What should you do if a Velociraptor hides in your potato patch?
Keep your eyes peeled.

Why shouldn't you keep your Brontosaurus in a marble cage?
It might roll away.

What happened when the Ultrasaurus joined the circus?
He carried the whole show.

How long will a dinosaur candle burn?
For a wick.

Where did Stegosaurus have their hair dyed?
In a tint.

How should you go hunting for a dinosaur
that's wearing a hat?
With a cap gun.

Why couldn't dinosaurs play the clarinet?
None of them could reed.

Why don't Dryosaurus like pogo sticks?
They make them feel jumpy.

What did Pterydactyl poets eat?
Rhyme bread.

What do you call a Triceratops that weaves
twill?
Materialistic.

Did you hear about the Tyrannosaurus
who forced a rabbit to sit on his head and
wave a fan all day?
He was hare conditioned.

How did the Carnosaurus get a job as a postmaster?
By stamping his feet.

What did the Triceratops have to do before he got a job with the railroad?
Take a training course.

Where did the Titanosaurus study to be an optometrist?
In the glassroom.

Where did the dinosaurs sit while doing their laundry?
On the bleachers.

How did the Allosaurus send her mother an umbrella?
By parasol post.

Was Gus a good card player?
Sure, he reached the pinochle of success.

31

Why didn't the dinosaurs keep calendars?
They didn't know their days were numbered.

Why didn't Gus remember to buy an axe?
He forgot to put it on his chopping list.

Why did Gus keep his watch on a chain?
So he could keep track of the time.

What kind of company makes tiny clocks shaped like dinosaurs?
Small-time operators.

When did the Brontosaurus's swim meet start?
At the stroke of ten.

What happened when Gus bought a pair of wooden shoes?
He lumbered around in them.

How did the Chinese dinosaurs cut down trees?
With chopsticks.

How much did the Chinese dinosaurs weigh?
Won ton.

How did the Camptosaurus open a flea market?
They started from scratch.

Why did the Allosaurus always carry a pair of tweezers?
In case she needed them in a pinch.

How did the Ceratops get rich in the soap business?
She bubbled her money.

What happened when Gus dropped out of the Memory Improvement Club?
He couldn't remember.

Why didn't Gus join Weight Watchers?
He thought it was a losing proposition.

What kind of dinosaurs hung out under trees?
The shady characters.

How did the Pterodactyls agree on the betting rules for their poker game?
They decided the sky was the limit.

What happened when the Tyrannosaurus was swallowed by a whale?
He was in a gnaw-ful predicament.

What happened to the Tyrannosaurus that ate a writer and got sick?
He came down with authoritis.

What did Gus the Goofasaurus say to his clock when it stopped?
"Tock to me!"

34

Did you hear about the Brontosaurus with lots of inhibitions?
He was tied up in nots.

Did you hear that everyone was ignoring the dinosaur who told dirty jokes?
He was obscene but not heard.

Why did the Tyrannosaurus eat the violin player?
She wanted to eliminate the fiddle man.

What did Gus the Goofasaurus say after he fixed the horn on his bicycle?
"Beep repaired."

Why did Gus eat oysters?
To develop mussel tone.

Why did Gus write out his tax return on Kleenex?
Because he knew he was going to have to pay through the nose.

What did Gus say to the quiet mouse?
"Squeak up!"

Why was Gus fired from his job as a gardener?
He was too rough around the hedges.

Did Gus become a doctor when he got a job as a soda jerk?
No, he became a fizzician.

Show me a Titanosaurus that works for the phone company and I'll show you a big operator.

Show me a statue of a talking dinosaur and I'll show you a figure of speech.

What did Mrs. Tyrannosaurus say to her lazy husband when a herd of Stegosaurus wandered by?
"Don't just stand there—slay something."

What happened to Humpty Dumpty after
the Tyrannosaurus attacked him?
He was a shell of his former self.

How do we know that Tyrannosaurus were
religious?
They were always saying "let us prey."

What happened to the dinosaur that ate
onions and beans?
She had tear gas.

Why did Gus think that his family tree
was a filbert tree?
Because it produced so many nuts.

What do you get when a Tyrannosaurus
attacks a newspaper?
You get an express.

Why was Gus fired from his job putting up
pictures at the museum?
He couldn't get the hang of it.

How did the Tin Man feel after his battle
with the Tyrannosaurus?
He was bent out of shape.

Did the Tyrannosaurus object to eating a
skeleton?
He made no bones about it.

Olive in Fear of Tyrannosaurus

Knock-knock.
Who's there?
Ima.
Ima who?
Ima 'fraid of dinosaurs.

Knock-knock.
Who's there?
Yura.
Yura who?
Yura dinosaur freak.

Knock-knock.
Who's there?
Millie.
Millie who?
Millie of years ago, dinosaurs roamed the earth.

Knock-knock.
Who's there?
Woody.
Woody who?
Woody you like a pet dinosaur?

Knock-knock.
Who's there?
Allah.
Allah who?
Allah the dinosaurs are extinct.

Knock-knock.
Who's there?
Yul.
Yul who?
Yul be sorry if you get eaten by a Tyrannosaurus.

Knock-knock.
Who's there?
Athena.
Athena who?
Athena dinosaur skeleton at the museum.

Knock-knock.
Who's there?
Luke.
Luke who?
Luke out for dinosaurs.

Knock-knock.
Who's there?
Hugh.
Hugh who?
Hugh'll find dinosaur fossils in Arizona.

Knock-knock.
Who's there?
Ira.
Ira who?
Ira my report on dinosaurs.

Knock-knock.
Who's there?
Alfie.
Alfie who?
Alfie your dinosaur while you're on vacation.

Knock-knock.
Who's there?
Dewey.
Dewey who?
Dewey know why dinosaurs are extinct?

Knock-knock.
Who's there?
Ty.
Ty who?
Tyrannosaurus!

Knock-knock.
Who's there?
Bianca.
Bianca who?
Biancasaurus.

Knock-knock.
Who's there?
Edward.
Edward who?
Edward like a dinosaur for his birthday.

Knock-knock.
Who's there?
Switch.
Switch who?
Switch is bigger, a Brontosaurus or an Ultrasaurus?

Knock-knock.
Who's there?
Osborn.
Osborn who?
Osborn two hundred million years after the dinosaurs.

Knock-knock.
Who's there?
Orange.
Orange who?
Orange you a dinosaur freak?

Knock-knock.
Who's there?
Omar.
Omar who?
Omar stars, there's a dinosaur outside.

Knock-knock.
Who's there?
Woodenshoe.
Woodenshoe who?
Woodenshoe like to have a dinosaur?

Knock-knock.
Who's there?
Usher.
Usher who?
Usher hope I don't meet a Tyrannosaurus.

Knock-knock.
Who's there?
Razor.
Razor who?
Razor pet dinosaur from an egg.

Knock-knock.
Who's there?
Avenue.
Avenue who?
Avenue heard, dinosaurs are extinct.

Knock-knock.
Who's there?
Lyndon.
Lyndon who?
Lyndon me your dinosaur would be a nice
thing to do.

Knock-knock.
Who's there?
Justice.
Justice who?
Justice I knocked on your door, a Tyrannosaurus bit me.

Knock-knock.
Who's there?
Hominy.
Hominy who?
Hominy dinosaur names do you know?

Knock-knock.
Who's there?
Rhoda.
Rhoda who?
Rhoda dinosaur over here from my house.

Knock-knock.
Who's there?
Dough.
Dough who?
Dough keep me waiting out here, there's a Tyrannosaurus on my tail.

Knock-knock.
Who's there?
Brawn.
Brawn who?
Brawn-tosaurus.

44

Knock-knock.
Who's there?
Stray.
Stray who?
Stray-gosaurus.

Knock-knock.
Who's there?
Tripe.
Tripe who?
Tripe-ceratops.

Knock-knock.
Who's there?
Tryin'.
Tryin' who?
Tryin'-asaurus Rex.

Knock-knock.
Who's there?
Scary.
Scary who?
Scary-dactyl.

Knock-knock.
Who's there?
Di.
Di who?
Dinosaur.

Knock-knock.
Who's there?
Samoa.
Samoa who?
Samoa dinosaurs.

Knock-knock.
Who's there?
Stella.
Stella who?
Stella nother dinosaur.

Knock-knock.
Who's there?
Consumption.
Consumption who?
Consumption make all these dinosaurs go away?

Knock-knock.
Who's there?
Goose.
Goose who?
Goose the dinosaurs at the museum.

Knock-knock.
Who's there?
Jewel.
Jewel who?
Jewel love all my dinosaur jokes.

Knock-knock.
Who's there?
Alda.
Alda who?
Alda dinosaurs are extinct.

Knock-knock.
Who's there?
Yacht.
Yacht who?
Yacht to learn some dinosaur jokes.

Knock-knock.
Who's there?
Dishes.
Dishes who?
Dishes not the Jurassic period.

Knock-knock.
Who's there?
Kent.
Kent who?
Kent you keep your dinosaur under control?

Knock-knock.
Who's there?
Snow.
Snow who?
Snow way I'd fight a Tyrannosaurus.

Knock-knock.
Who's there?
One.
One who?
One-der why the dinosaurs are dead.

Knock-knock.
Who's there?
Cozy.
Cozy who?
Cozy if the Tyrannosaurus has gone away.

Knock-knock.
Who's there?
Detail.
Detail who?
Detail of an Ultrasaurus was twenty feet
long.

Knock-knock.
Who's there?
Alien.
Alien who?
Alientologists study dinosaur fossils.

Knock-knock.
Who's there?
Alan.
Alan who?
Alan my stuffed dinosaur to Harry.

Knock-knock.
Who's there?
Anita.
Anita who?
Anita book on dinosaurs for my report.

Knock-knock.
Who's there?
Foster.
Foster who?
Foster than a speeding Pterodactyl.

Knock-knock.
Who's there?
Daryl.
Daryl who?
Daryl never be another dinosaur.

Knock-knock.
Who's there?
Fanny.
Fanny who?
Fanny Tyrannosaurus knock, don't let them in.

Knock-knock.
Who's there?
Harold.
Harold who?
Harold is that dinosaur egg?

Knock-knock.
Who's there?
Jack.
Jack who?
Jack for dinosaurs before you go into the cave.

Knock-knock.
Who's there?
Joe Namath.
Joe Namath who?
Joe Namathn't Tyrannosaurus Rex, is it?

Knock-knock.
Who's there?
Juliet.
Juliet who?
Juliet dinosaur eggs.

Knock-knock.
Who's there?
Kenneth.
Kenneth who?
Kenneth be a dinosaur fossil?

Knock-knock.
Who's there?
Mandy.
Mandy who?
Mandy guns, the Tyrannosaurus are charging!

Knock-knock.
Who's there?
Matthew.
Matthew who?
Matthew is made from dinosaur leather.

Knock-knock.
Who's there?
Norman.
Norman who?
Norman has ever seen a live dinosaur.

Knock-knock.
Who's there?
Olive.
Olive who?
Olive in fear of Tyrannosaurus.

Knock-knock.
Who's there?
Oliver.
Oliver who?
Oliver dinosaurs have escaped.

Knock-knock.
Who's there?
Phineas.
Phineas who?
Phineas dinosaurs were the Goofasaurus.

Knock-knock.
Who's there?
Seymour.
Seymour who?
Seymour dinosaurs at the museum?

Knock-knock.
Who's there?
Stefan.
Stefan who?
Stefan the gas, there's a Tyrannosaurus chasing us.

Knock-knock.
Who's there?
Tobias.
Tobias who?
Tobias a dinosaur will cost a lot of money.

Knock-knock.
Who's there?
Wayne.
Wayne who?
Wayne did dinosaurs roam the earth?

Knock-knock.
Who's there?
Canoe.
Canoe who?
Canoe name seven kinds of dinosaurs?

Knock-knock.
Who's there?
Oswald.
Oswald who?
Oswald my tongue when I saw that Tyrannosaurus.

Knock-knock.
Who's there?
Zephyr.
Zephyr who?
Zephyr the army, the dinosaurs are invading!

Knock-knock.
Who's there?
Twain.
Twain who?
Twain your dinosaur not to bite!

Knock-knock.
Who's there?
Bart.
Bart who?
Bart-ender, a ginger ale for my Brontosaurus.

Knock-knock.
Who's there?
Lass.
Lass who?
Lass-o a dinosaur and you'll be famous.

Knock-knock.
Who's there?
Juan.
Juan who?
Juan hundred million years ago, dino-
saurs were already extinct.

Knock-knock.
Who's there?
Tuba.
Tuba who?
Tuba a dinosaur costs too much money.

Knock-knock.
Who's there?
X.
X who?
X was how dinosaurs had babies.

Knock-knock.
Who's there?
Armageddon.
Armageddon who?
Armageddon a new dinosaur book.

Knock-knock.
Who's there?
Dinosaur.
Dinosaur who?
Dinosaur is a famous singer.

Knock-knock.
Who's there?
Disaster.
Disaster who?
Disaster be my favorite dinosaur book.

Knock-knock.
Who's there?
Disguise.
Disguise who?
Disguise a dinosaur nut!

Knock-knock.
Who's there?
Element.
Element who?
Element to buy a dog, but she got a dinosaur instead.

Knock-knock.
Who's there?
Formosa.
Formosa who?
Formosa their lives, dinosaurs hungry.

55

Knock-knock.
Who's there?
Halibut.
Halibut who?
Halibut some dinosaur jokes?

Knock-knock.
Who's there?
Ivory.
Ivory who?
Ivory afraid of Tyrannosaurus.

Knock-knock.
Who's there?
Mica.
Mica who?
Mica was crushed by a Titanosaurus.

Knock-knock.
Who's there?
Miniature.
Miniature who?
Miniature attacked by a Carnosaurus, you're doomed.

Knock-knock.
Who's there?
Virtue.
Virtue who?
Virtue attacked by a Tyrannosaurus?

Knock-knock.
Who's there?
Dishes.
Dishes who?
Dishes a Tyrannosaurus, open up!

Knock-knock.
Who's there?
Lettuce.
Lettuce who?
Lettuce hope the Tyrannosaurus can't get in.

Knock-knock.
Who's there?
Mavis.
Mavis who?
Mavis be the last time a Tyrannosaurus knocks at our door.

Knock-knock.
Who's there?
Thistle.
Thistle who?
Thistle be our last day on earth if that Tyrannosaurus gets in!

Knock-knock.
Who's there?
Eggs.
Eggs who?
Eggstremely unlikely that we can escape
this Tyrannosaurus.

Knock-knock.
Who's there?
Waddle.
Waddle who?
Waddle we do if the Tyrannosaurus
catches us?

Knock-knock.
Who's there?
Heywood.
Heywood who?
Heywood you stop talking about that Ty-
rannosaurus, you're making me nervous.

Knock-knock.
Who's there?
Havelock.
Havelock who?
Havelock put on your door and we won't
have to worry about Tyrannosaurus.

Knock-knock.
Who's there?
Tillie.
Tillie who?
Tillie Tyrannosaurus goes away, I'm hiding.

Knock-knock.
Who's there?
Olga.
Olga who?
Olga out and see if the Tyrannosaurus's gone.

Knock-knock.
Who's there?
Juan.
Juan who?
Juan wrong move and that Tyrannosaurus will get you.

Knock-knock.
Who's there?
Xavier.
Xavier who?
Xavier self and run away from that Tyrannosaurus.

Knock-knock.
Who's there?
Isadore.
Isadore who?
Isadore any barrier to a Tyrannosaurus?

Knock-knock.
Who's there?
Savannah.
Savannah who?
Savannah you going to try to escape that Tyrannosaurus?

Knock-knock.
Who's there?
Ken.
Ken who?
Ken a Tyrannosaurus fit in your living room?

Knock-knock.
Who's there?
Justice.
Justice who?
Justice I got away from that Tyrannosaurus, another one found me!

Knock-knock.
Who's there?
Sincerely.
Sincerely who?
Sincerely this morning I've been chased by
Tyrannosaurus.

Knock-knock.
Who's there?
Asher.
Asher who?
Asher would like to escape these hungry
Tyrannosaurus.

Knock-knock.
Who's there?
Betty.
Betty who?
Betty not let those Tyrannosaurus catch
you.

Knock-knock.
Who's there?
Freighter.
Freighter who?
Freighter Tyrannosaurus? You bet I am!

Knock-knock.
Who's there?
Emmett.
Emmett who?
Emmett the end of my patience with these Tyrannosaurus.

Knock-knock.
Who's there?
Olga.
Olga who?
Olga to the ends of the earth to avoid a Tyrannosaurus.

Knock-knock.
Who's there?
Ice cream.
Ice cream who?
Ice cream when I see a Tyrannosaurus.

Knock-knock.
Who's there?
Howell.
Howell who?
Howell I ever escape these Tyrannosau-rus?

Knock-knock.
Who's there?
Ali.
Ali who?
Ali-luyah, the Tyrannosaurus have gone away.

Knock-knock.
Who's there?
Norma Lee.
Norma Lee who?
Norma Lee Tyrannosaurus do not attack people.

Knock-knock.
Who's there?
Ann.
Ann who?
Ann angry Tyrannosaurus will attack anything.

Knock-knock.
Who's there?
Madam.
Madam who?
Madam luck, a Tyrannosaurus found me.

Knock-knock.
Who's there?
Musket.
Musket who?
Musket away from a hungry Tyrannosaurus.

Knock-knock.
Who's there?
Butter.
Butter who?
Butter hide from that Tyrannosaurus.

Knock-knock.
Who's there?
Yelp.
Yelp who?
Yelp me hide from that Tyrannosaurus.

Knock-knock.
Who's there?
Gutter.
Gutter who?
Gutter find a place where Tyrannosaurus won't follow me.

Knock-knock.
Who's there?
Ken.
Ken who?
Ken I hide from the Tyrannosaurus in your basement?

Knock-knock.
Who's there?
Wanda.
Wanda who?
Wanda if Tyrannosaurus like garlic.

Knock-knock.
Who's there?
Razor.
Razor who?
Razor children to avoid Tyrannosaurus.

Knock-knock.
Who's there?
Colin.
Colin who?
Colin all cars, Tyrannosaurus on the loose!

Knock-knock.
Who's there?
Iris.
Iris who?
Iris the police would catch those Tyrannosaurus.

Knock-knock.
Who's there?
Toyota.
Toyota who?
Toyota be some protection against hungry dinosaurs.

Knock-knock.
Who's there?
Izzy.
Izzy who?
Izzy Tyrannosaurus gone?

Knock-knock.
Who's there?
Omar.
Omar who?
Omar goodness, now there are five Tyran-
nosaurus outside.

Knock-knock.
Who's there?
Odette.
Odette who?
Odette's a bad sign when five Tyrannosau-
rus want to eat you.

Knock-knock.
Who's there?
Les.
Les who?
Les give the Tyrannosaurus some bologna
instead.

Knock-knock.
Who's there?
Thad.
Thad who?
Thad'll never satisfy a hungry Tyranno-
saurus.

Knock-knock.
Who's there?
Donut.
Donut who?
Donut think I'll ever escape these Tyran-
nosaurus now.

Knock-knock.
Who's there?
Donalette.
Donalette who?
Donalette those Tyrannosaurus eat me, I
beg you.

Knock-knock.
Who's there?
Fido.
Fido who?
Fido I have these Tyrannosaurus after me?

67

Knock-knock.
Who's there?
Tank.
Tank who?
Tank heavens Tyrannosaurus don't carry guns!

Knock-knock.
Who's there?
Hymie.
Hymie who?
Hymie from those Tyrannosaurus.

Knock-knock.
Who's there?
Closure.
Closure who?
Closure eyes and maybe the Tyrannosaurus will go away.

Knock-knock.
Who's there?
Noah.
Noah who?
Noah such luck, the Tyrannosaurus are still here.

Knock-knock.
Who's there?
Alec.
Alec who?
Alec Triceratops, not Tyrannosaurus.

Knock-knock.
Who's there?
Wiener.
Wiener who?
Wiener the police going to get these Ty-
rannosaurus out of here?

Knock-knock.
Who's there?
Lewis.
Lewis who?
Lewis in all hope of being saved from these
Tyrannosaurus.

Knock-knock.
Who's there?
Mae.
Mae who?
Maebe Superman will save me from these
Tyrannosaurus.

Knock-knock.
Who's there?
Adlai.
Adlai who?
Adlai a bet that Superman is afraid of them too.

Knock-knock.
Who's there?
Jaws.
Jaws who?
Jaws truly is scared of Tyrannosaurus.

Knock-knock.
Who's there?
Annetta.
Annetta who?
Annetta day of being chased by Tyrannosaurus and I'll go crazy.

Knock-knock.
Who's there?
Haydn.
Haydn who?
Haydn from Tyrannosaurus is no fun.

Knock-knock.
Who's there?
Osborn.
Osborn who?
Osborn to be eaten by Tyrannosaurus.

Knock-knock.
Who's there?
Loch.
Loch who?
Loch and see if the Tyrannosaurus have left.

Knock-knock.
Who's there?
Steel.
Steel who?
Steel five Tyrannosaurus outside.

Knock-knock.
Who's there?
Amory.
Amory who?
Amory Christmas this'll be if the Tyrannosaurus get me.

Knock-knock.
Who's there?
Gilda.
Gilda who?
Gilda Tyrannosaurus before they kill me.

Knock-knock.
Who's there?
Datsun.
Datsun who?
Datsun big ugly Tyrannosaurus waiting for me outside.

Knock-knock.
Who's there?
Ollie.
Ollie who?
Ollie can think about is those hungry Tyrannosaurus.

Knock-knock.
Who's there?
Hominy.
Hominy who?
Hominy Tyrannosaurus outside now?

Knock-knock.
Who's there?
Eva.
Eva who?
Eva more Tyrannosaurus than the last time I looked.

Knock-knock.
Who's there?
Meg.
Meg who?
Meg sure you don't let those Tyrannosaurus in.

Knock-knock.
Who's there?
Alison.
Alison who?
Alison the Tyrannosaurus want to eat me.

Knock-knock.
Who's there?
Fodder.
Fodder who?
Fodder last time, don't let those Tyrannosaurus in!

Knock-knock.
Who's there?
Zoo.
Zoo who?
Zoo don't want to be eaten by Tyrannosaurus.

Knock-knock.
Who's there?
Cindy.
Cindy who?
Cindy army in if the police can't stop the Tyrannosaurus.

Knock-knock.
Who's there?
Emma.
Emma who?
Emma going to be a Tyrannosaurus's dinner?

Knock-knock.
Who's there?
Hollis.
Hollis who?
Hollis lost if the Tyrannosaurus get me.

Knock-knock.
Who's there?
Wicked.
Wicked who?
Wicked escape the Tyrannosaurus if you had a tank.

74

Knock-knock.
Who's there?
Eyesore.
Eyesore who?
Eyesore am tired of these Tyrannosaurus

Knock-knock.
Who's there?
Guinevere.
Guinevere who?
Guinevere these Tyrannosaurus go away,
I'll give you a big kiss.

Knock-knock.
Who's there?
Anthem.
Anthem who?
Anthem men are always chased by Tyran-
nosaurus.

Knock-knock.
Who's there?
Gwen.
Gwen who?
Gwen will the Tyrannosaurus leave me
alone?

75

Knock-knock.
Who's there?
Congo.
Congo who?
Congo on much longer hiding from these
Tyrannosaurus.

A Few Good Dinosaurs

What do you call a dinosaur that takes things without realizing it?
A Kleptosaurus!

Eenie, meenie, minie, mo,
Catch a dinosaur by the toe,
When she hollers,
Run!

How many dinosaurs choose a medical career?
Fortunately, very few!

Why did many Tyrannosaurus play musical instruments?
They had a talent for it!

Why don't dinosaurs like to go to the movies?
The seats are murder on their tails!

Why don't many dinosaurs become actors?
Their eyes are very sensitive to bright
lights!

Which days of the week are baby dinosaurs allowed to play?
Every day!

What do you call a dinosaur in a treetop?
Ridiculous!

Why did the dinosaur go to the market?
Because the little piggy had to stay home!

What do you get when you cross a Pterodactyl with a teddy bear?
A cuddlysaurus!

Where do you buy presents for a baby dinosaur?
At Dino-Tots!

Why don't dinosaurs wear wrist watches?
Because they only have legs!

What do you call a dinosaur who owns a fleet of ships?
Rich!

What do you get when you cross a Brontosaurus and a Greek person?
A dinosaur that craves feta cheese and olives!

How do dinosaurs kiss?
With their lips, silly!

Name a famous American dinosaur that won the Tchaikovsky Piano Competition in the Triassic period.
Van Cliburnosaurus!

Name a famous American dinosaur composer from the Jurassic period.
Leonard Bernsteinosaurus!

Why didn't the dinosaur help Humpty Dumpty after he fell?
If all the king's horses and all the king's men couldn't help, why bother?

Why don't dinosaurs like to swim?
Bathing suits rarely allow for tail room!

What do you get when you cross a Triceratops with a horse?
A loyal dinosaur!

Why don't dinosaurs have big weddings?
Seating arrangements are impossible!

What do you get when you cross a Teratosaurus with a cow?
A lazy dinosaur that gives milk!

What do you call an English dinosaur?
A Britosaurus!

What do you get when you cross a dinosaur with a spider?
An amazing web!

What do you call a Diplodocus interested in fashion?
A designosaurus!

Why don't dinosaurs like to knit?
They find it difficult to maneuver the needles!

What do you call dinosaurs that enjoy afternoon tea?
Civilized!

What do you get when you cross a goose with a Tyrannosaurus?
Dinosaur pillows!

Why don't dinosaurs like to curtsy?
It hurts their knees!

What is the difference between girl dinosaurs and boy dinosaurs?
It's elementary!

Where are dinosaurs buried?
In the ground!

What do you call a dinosaur that comes from a royal family?
Your majesty!

What do baby dinosaurs wear?
Pamposaurs!

What do you get when you cross a Ceratosaurus and a lamb?
A soft dinosaur!

Name a famous baseball dinosaur.
Mickey Mantlesaurus!

What do you call a dinosaur that likes velvet?
Chic!

The dinosaur in the wilderness asked me,
"How many blueberries grow in the sea?"
I answered him as best I could:
"As many fish as grow in the woods!"

What do you call a dinosaur successful in business?
An entrepreneurosaurus!

What do you call a dinosaur that enjoys babysitting?
A Nanosaurus!

What do you call a dinosaur and a cat that spend a lot of time together?
Best buddies!

There once was a dull dinosaur,
Who suffered from being a bore.
His looks weren't flawed,
He was perfectly clawed.
But he sure made everyone snore!

Once there was a dinosaur,
Who wore a cute hat,
As black as a cat,
And his legs were very, very fat!

Dinosaurs growl,
Dinosaurs bite.
I hide all day,
And run all night.
Never to let a dinosaur bite!

What do you call large dinosaur eggs?
Jumbo!

What do you do when you find a dinosaur
egg?
Prepare a large omelette!

What do you call a dinosaur that has a
backbone, breathes air, has a scaly body
covering and isn't a crocodile, an alligator,
a turtle, a snake, or a lizard?
Obviously, a dinosaur!

Name a famous Hungarian musical dinosaur.
Lisztosaurus!

Did you hear what happened to Norman while working on his dinosaur movie script?
The computer grew scales!

What do you get when you cross an Orodromeus with Popeye?
A dinosaur that craves spinach!

What did the American Museum of Natural History expedition do after discovering the remains of two baby dinosaurs in Mongolia?
They celebrated!

What does a Psittacosaurus do to stop grinding his teeth?
He wears a bite plate!

Why don't dinosaurs like to wear braces?
They hate it when food gets caught!

What tastes good on a juicy steak?
Mussaurus sauce!

What do you call a dinosaur that graduates from an Ivy League college?
A Yaleosaurus!

Knock-knock.
Who's there?
Erectopus.
Erectopus who?
Erectopus Rex!

Knock-knock.
Who's there?
Iggy and Don.
Iggy and Don who?
Iguanodon!

What do you call a dinosaur that lives in Las Vegas?
A gamblasaurus!

What do you call a mechanical dinosaur?
A robotasaurus!

What do you call a dinosaur that repairs heating systems?
A plumbersaurus!

What do you get when you cross a washing machine with an Apatosaurus?
A very clean dinosaur!

What is the favorite reference book for Jurassic singers?
An operasaurus!

What is the name of the famous opera from the Triassic period?
Aidasaurus!

What is the name of a famous piece of dinosaur music based on a poem by the German writer Goethe?
The Steneosaurus's Apprentice!

What is a famous dinosaur operetta?
Pirates of Pinacosaurus!

Why didn't the Ceratosaurus like to practice the piano?
He doesn't like to play with scales!

What is a famous dinosaur musical?
The Sound of Mussaurus!

What do you get when you cross a dyslexic Danubiosaurus with a turtle?
A slow dinosaur that has difficulty reading!

What do you get when you cross a Helopus with a Bactrosaurus?
An unusual dinosaur!

What is the name of a famous scientific dinosaur movie?
The Orodromeus Strain!

Name the famous dinosaur queen who was sent to the guillotine.
Marie Antoinetteasaurus!

Who is the favorite twentieth-century purple and green dinosaur?
Barney!

What happens to dinosaurs who drink too much alcohol?
They get Ceratosaurus of the liver!

Name the famous Viennese dinosaur waltz.
The Blue Danubiosaurus!

What do you get when you cross a Lesothosaurus with a helicopter?
A dinosaur with bizarre ears!

DINOSAUR ONE: How do you get three proper elderly Sauropods to curse?
DINOSAUR TWO: I don't know. How?
DINOSAUR ONE: You get a fourth one to yell "bingo!"

Which group of dinosaurs believe in mummification?
The Aegyptosaurus!

What problem do baby dinosaurs often have?
Saur-throats!

DINOSAUR ONE: "Have you ever been to this doctor before?"

DINOSAUR TWO: "No. I never needed an orthopedist."

DINOSAUR DOCTOR: "Please come in." (pointing to Dinosaur One)

Dinosaur One proceeds very slowly, walking hunched over close to the floor, and in pain. One half hour later, he finally enters the doctor's office. A few minutes later, he comes out of the doctor's office, erect and walking like a young dinosaur.

DINOSAUR TWO: "Doctor, it's a miracle. What is your secret?"

DINOSAUR DOCTOR: "Very simple. I gave him a longer cane!"

Why don't they have dinosaurs in any of the famous zoos?
Guess!

BABY DINOSAUR: "Can I go out and play?"

MOTHER DINOSAUR: "No."

BABY DINOSAUR: "Why not?"

MOTHER DINOSAUR: "It's too late."

BABY DINOSAUR: "Too late for what?"

MOTHER DINOSAUR: "Too late to go out and play!"

What do you have when your Pterodactyl
falls down a flight of stairs?
A problem!

What's the difference between a Steneosaurus and a Diplodocus?
The spelling!

What should you do with an eighteen-year-
old Crocodilia?
Send her to college!

How do you roast a dinosaur?
By gathering all his friends!

What do you get when you cross a Pinacosaurus with a fish?
The first dinosaur to enter the Olympic
swimming competition!

What kind of dinosaurs go to doctors all
the time?
Hypochondriasaurus.

What do you give an Apatosaurus that cannot breathe?
Oxygen!

Why do dinosaurs generally have elaborate weddings?
Because they cantaloupe!

Why do dinosaurs prefer swimming in the ocean rather than a pool?
More room!

What do you get when you cross a Sauropod with Bugs Bunny?
A dinosaur that likes carrots!

What do you call it when a dinosaur accomplishes something spectacular?
A tour de saur!

What do dinosaurs like to eat with their coffee?
Dinonuts!

What is a popular Tyrannosaurus toothpaste?
Dinodent!

How do left-handed dinosaurs cut paper?
With scissors!

What do dinosaurs like to watch on television?
Dinotoons!

Why aren't dinosaurs used to pull
wagons?
Their tails block the view of the driver!

If you saw a group of dinosaurs walking
down the street with tennis rackets, what
would you do?
Laugh!

What do you have when you cross a dinosaur with a bus?
A pollution problem!

What do you have when you cross a dinosaur with a vampire?
A blood shortage!

Where do dinosaurs learn to read?
In school, where else?

What do you get when a dinosaur skydives?
A large crater!

What do you get when you cross a Jurassic Stenosaurus with paper?
A library!

What do you call dinosaurs that drive limousines?
Chauffeurs!

Norman the Triceratops was attracted to Violet the Velociraptor, who ignored him. Finally, he confronted her one day and demanded to know why she continually ignored him. "Sorry," said the Velociraptor, "but I'm only interested in Velociraptors!"

What is a favorite dinosaur vegetable?
Broccoliosaurus!

Why do dinosaurs avoid haircuts?
Because they don't have any hair!

What did the Barapasaurus say to the Avisaurus?
We'll never know!

Why did the dinosaurs from the Triassic period eat so little?
They were always on diets!

Why did the Tyrannosaurus eat a knife?
He wanted to cut out fat from his diet!

Why did Gus the Goofasaurus cover the coffee cup before heating it in the microwave oven?
He wanted to protect the coffee from those dangerous microwaves!

What did the feminist Mussasaurus say to the male Allosaurus?
If you prefer Hanes, wear them!

Why do dinosaurs avoid dates?
Because they're partial to bananas!

How late do dinosaurs sleep in the morning?
As late as they want!

What do you call a dinosaur from Russia?
A Cossackosaurus!

Why did the Ceratosaurus lose the relay race?
Because they didn't run fast enough!

Why don't dinosaurs work in construction?
Hard hats don't fit well!

Have you heard about the new movie directed by Tyrannosaurus Rex?
No. What is the name of it?
A Few Good Dinosaurs!

Have you heard about the new dinosaur music, theater, and dance complex?
It's called Lincoln Center for the Pterodactyl Arts!

Have you heard about the famous, slightly off-beat chef on television?
He's known as the Galloping Gorgasaurus!

Name the famous Dravidosaurus chef who has written many cookbooks.
Marcella Hazanosaurus!

DINOSAUR ONE: "How do I get to Carnegie Hall?"
DINOSAUR TWO: "Practice!"

What is the worst problem for aging dinosaurs?
False teeth!

What kind of sneakers are popular in the dinosaur community?
Nikeopods!

Where do dinosaurs prefer to dine?
At home!

Did you hear about the popular dinosaur moving company?
The Seven Steneosaurus Brothers!

What do you call a dinosaur that only eats vegetables?
Deprived!

What is the name of the famous Civil War dinosaur movie?
Gone With the Helopus!

DINOSAUR ONE: "I want a divorce."
DINOSAUR TWO: "Why?"
DINOSAUR ONE: "I need to move on."
DINOSAUR TWO: "Why?"
DINOSAUR ONE: "It's time."
DINOSAUR TWO: "Why?"
DINOSAUR ONE: "I think it's obvious!"

What is a favorite dinosaur soft drink?
Saursparilla!

Why did the Brontosaurus stick to his guns?
He swallowed Krazy Glue!

What shouldn't you do if you see a dinosaur?
Snap a photograph!

What kind of exercise equipment do Sauropods like to use?
The Nordicasaurus Track!

Which restaurant caters to dinosaurs?
The Four Albisauruses!

What do paleontologists do for relaxation?
Nothing. They're workaholics!

What do dinosaurs do in the sun?
Get burned!

Name a famous springtime dinosaur visitor.
The Easter Bunnypod!

What do dinosaurs eat at Passover?
Matzoh, of course!

How do dinosaurs prepare for bedtime?
First they take a bath and then they brush their teeth!

Where do the Marshosauruses prefer to picnic?
In a swamp!

Where do dinosaurs go if they have gum trouble?
To the periodontisaurus!

The dinosaur edition of *The New York Times* boasts "all the news that's fit to bite!"

Why were Triceratops terrible explorers?
No sense of adventure!

Who is able to leap tall buildings and fly through the air?
Superdino!

How can you tell if there's an Iguanodon in your closet?
The door won't close!

Why don't dinosaurs take aerobics classes?
Weak knees!

What should you do if a dinosaur wants to borrow your homework?
Insist that he keep it!

Dinosaur Soup

Two dinosaurs met at a watering hole in the jungle and started talking. "Hey," said the first one, "did you hear the one about the Goofasaurus who was so stu—"

"Stop right there!" shouted the second dinosaur. "I happen to be a Goofasaurus!"

"Gee, sorry," said the first dinosaur. "I hadn't noticed. Okay ... so ... did ... you ... hear ... the ... one ... about ... the ... Goofasaurus ... who ... was ... so ... stupid ..."

Mrs. Miller was very worried when her husband came home late from his weekly golf game. He arrived looking very tired and dirty. "What happened?" she cried.

"It was terrible," Mr. Miller said. "Hank and I were just teeing off when a Brontosaurus burst out of the woods with a Tyrannosaurus right behind it. They came right for us. I managed to get out of the way, but Hank wasn't fast enough. They ran right over him and he died right there."

"How awful!"

"I know. All day long it was hit the ball, drag Hank, hit the ball, drag Hank."

Bill worked at the zoo where he was in charge of feeding the Tyrannosaurus. He began to have a terrible urge to stick his hand in one of the dinosaur's mouth. So he decided to go see a psychiatrist to cure him of his urge.

He told Dr. Freud about his problem and asked what he should do. Dr. Freud said, "I had a patient once who had an uncontrollable urge to put his hand in a pot of boiling water. He finally did, and he burned himself. But he never had the urge to do it again. Perhaps if you gave in to your urge just once, it would teach you never to do so again."

Bill agreed to take the doctor's advice and left.

The next day Dr. Freud's phone rang. "It's Bill," said the voice on the line. "I did what you said and put my hand in the Tyrannosaurus's mouth."

"What happened?"

"Well," said Bill. "We both got fired."

A Coelurus, a Dryosaurus, and a Goofasaurus are walking through the jungle at night when they hear a tremendous crashing behind them. They know that it is a pack of hungry Tyrannosaurus. They start running, but they can hear the Tyrannosaurus gaining on them.

"Quick," says the Coelurus. "Climb a tree. In the dark they won't be able to see us."

So each one climbs a different tree. Just then the pack of Tyrannosaurus arrives. They stop in front of the first tree. "They were here just a second ago," says one Tyrannosaur. "Maybe they're up in these trees."

He walks over and shakes the tree where the Coelurus is hiding.

"Whoo! Whoo!" calls the Coelurus.

"It's just an owl," says the Tyrannosaurus. "Let's try the next tree."

He shakes the tree where the Dryosaurus is hiding.

"Caw! Caw!" cries the Dryosaurus.

"Just a crow," grumbles the Tyrannosaurus. And he moves on to the third tree, where the Goofasaurus is hiding.

He shakes the tree.

And from the darkness above comes, "Moo! Moo!"

An Allosaurus and a Goofasaurus meet at a watering hole. The Allosaurus has a wooden leg, and the Goofasaurus has a glass eye and a hook where his hand should be.

"How did you get that hook?" asks the Allosaurus.

"I was chased by a Tyrannosaurus," says the Goofasaurus. "He caught my hand in his mouth and bit it off, but I managed to escape. The next day, I had this hook put on. How did you lose your leg?"

"I was caught by a Carnosaurus. He bit off my leg, and while he was eating it, I was able to limp off. How did you lose your eye?"

"I don't want to talk about it," says the Goofasaurus.

"Come on, it can't be that bad," says the Allosaurus. "We've both survived some pretty awful stuff."

"Okay," says the Goofasaurus. "One day, I got some mud in my eye."

"That's all? Mud shouldn't cause you to lose your eye."

"I know," says the Goofasaurus. "But it was the first day I had my hook."

A few days later the Allosaurus ran into the Goofasaurus again. The Goofasaurus was holding a mouse in front of his mouth.

"What are you doing?"

"A bird flew down my throat. I'm trying to get it out."

"But birds don't like mice," the Allosaurus pointed out.

"I know," said the Goofasaurus. "But first I have to get out the cat that chased the bird in."

Amy's pet dinosaur died, and she wanted to give it a funeral. So her father dug a big hole in the backyard to bury him.

"Maybe you should say a little prayer," her father said.

"Okay," Amy said. "I bury you in the name of the Father and the Son—and into the hole he goes."

Louisa went to an auction where a talking Diplodocus was for sale. She bid and bid, but the price kept going up. Finally, she won the auction.

"This dinosaur had better talk for real," she told the auctioneer.

"Of course it does," said the auctioneer. "Who do you think was bidding against you?"

Leroy had a problem with the cats outside his house. All night long they made a terrible racket, crying and meowing. So he bought a Tyrannosaurus and put it in his yard.

That night he slept like a baby. There was no noise in the backyard. When he got up the next morning, he smiled and said, "No mews is good mews."

Benny's Ultrasaurus was sick, so he took it to the vet. "Doctor," he said, "will you treat my dinosaur?"

"Of course not," snapped the vet. "He has to pay, just like anyone else."

Clarice went to visit her cousin Andy in the jungle. There were dinosaurs everywhere, even in the house.

"There are so many of those nasty beasts," said Clarice. "Why don't you shoo them?"

"Silly," said Andrew. "Dinosaurs are supposed to be bare foot."

Ralph raised his hand in class. "Teacher, were there any dinosaurs on Noah's ark?"

"No, I don't think so," the teacher smiled.

"No wonder they're extinct."

"I hear your Diplodocus had an accident," said Moe.

"It did," said Curly. "It got loose and wandered downtown and walked in the back door of the Whiteside Theater. It wandered out on the proscenium, but it was so heavy that the floor broke and it fell into the basement."

"Are you going to punish it for running away?"

"Nah, it's just a stage it was going through."

Martha was walking through the park with her pet Dryosaurus when she ran into Dim Jim.

"I haven't seen you in ten years," Jim exclaimed. "And you still have the same dinosaur. Except he used to be a lot bigger."

"That was a different dinosaur. In fact, it was a Tyrannosaurus," replied Martha wearily.

"Gosh, you must have put him on a heck of a diet."

Betty ran into Alice one night walking a Brontosaurus and carrying a knitting needle.

"Why are you carrying that needle?" asked Betty.

"I use it to tell time," said Alice.

"How?"

Alice took the needle and gave the Brontosaurus a poke in the leg. The great beast let out a huge roar.

Suddenly, a window opened up down the street, and a man yelled, "Can't you keep that animal quiet? It's eleven-thirty!"

Dim Jim watched as Louie's pet Hadrosaurus played fetch.

"I had a dinosaur once, but I couldn't teach it to do anything," Dim Jim complained.

"It's easy to teach a dinosaur," Louie smiled. "But first you have to know more than it does."

Sally walked over to Louie a little later. "You know, your dinosaur bit my big brother yesterday."

Louie sighed. "I suppose you're going to ask me to pay the doctor bill."

"No," Sally said. "How much will it cost me to buy him from you?"

Mike went to the barber to get a haircut. In the corner there was a huge, slobbering Tyrannosaurus. He watched carefully as the barber cut Mike's hair.

"I didn't think a dinosaur would be so interested in a haircut," Mike said.

"He isn't," replied the barber. "It's just that sometimes I cut off someone's ear."

Tran went to visit his friend Chris in the hospital. "What happened?" he asked.

"I was walking down the street when a ferocious Carnosaurus jumped out in front of me. I read in a book that if a wild animal attacks you, you're supposed to stare it right in the eyes and it will back down. So I stared right at him."

"But it obviously didn't work," Tran pointed out.

"No," sighed Chris. "I guess that Carnosaurus hadn't read the book."

Joan was walking along the river when she ran into Bette, who was sitting on the back of an Ultrasaurus.

"What an ugly beast," Joan sniffed.

"He's quite handsome," Bette retorted. "And very strong. Why, I'll bet you that he can jump across the river."

"Cannot!" Joan challenged.

"Watch," said Bette. And she rode the dinosaur across the river and to the other bank. When it got there, it jumped.

Bob the accountant was having a terrible time going to sleep. He went to see his doctor. "Listen, I've got a great remedy," she told him. "Try counting dinosaurs."

"Dinosaurs?" said Bob.

"Believe me, it works," the doctor assured him.

Bob went home and tried it. For a few days everything was okay, but on Thursday he called his doctor again.

"What's wrong? Counting dinosaurs works for everybody who tries it," she said.

"It worked the first three nights," the tired accountant replied. "But then I made a mistake on Tuesday, and I've been up the past two nights trying to find it."

The plane was flying along at forty thousand feet when all of a sudden there was a tremendous crash from the cargo hold. The passengers started to panic, and it got even worse when there was another crash followed by a terrible roar. People were jumping out of their seats and yelling at the flight attendants.

Suddenly the door to the cockpit opened and the pilot came out. He looked so calm that everybody thought there couldn't be anything to worry about.

"You will all be okay. We have a little problem because a Tyrannosaurus that we are transporting to the Cincinnati zoo has escaped from his cage. But we have matters under control."

People sat down and began to relax. But then they noticed that the pilot had taken a pack out of a closet and was strapping it to his back.

"Hey! That's a parachute!" shouted one man. "You're deserting us."

"No, I'm not," said the pilot. "I'm going to get help."

Chris was in the hospital again, and Tran came to see him once more. "What happened this time?" Tran asked.

"That same dinosaur jumped me again. But I'd been reading up on boxing. So I gave him a right cross. Then I gave him a left cross."

"Then what happened?" Tran asked.

"Then came the Red Cross."

"Do you sell dinosaur's meat?" Mr. Fuddy asked the butcher.

"Of course not," the butcher replied. "How would they pay for it?"

Mr. Fuddy was always asking silly questions. He went to the pet store and said, "I'd like a dinosaur, please."

"I'm sorry, sir," the clerk told him. "But we have no dinosaurs."

"I'd like a dinosaur, please," Mr. Fuddy said again.

"I'm sorry, sir, but as I told you, we have no dinosaurs," the clerk repeated.

"I'd like a dinosaur, please," Mr. Fuddy persisted.

"Look, buddy," the clerk said. "If you took the ice out of ice cream, what would you have?"

"Cream," said Mr. Fuddy.

"And if you took the base out of baseball, what would you have?"

"Ball," said Mr. Fuddy.

"And if you took the bloom out of dinosaurs, what would you have?"

"There's no bloom in dinosaurs!" said Mr. Fuddy.

"That's what I'm trying to tell you! There ain't no bloomin' dinosaurs!"

Millie was visiting Janet's house when Janet started to feed their Tyrannosaurus peanut butter-and-jelly sandwiches.

"I didn't think Tyrannosaurus liked peanut butter and jelly," said Millie.

"They don't," Janet said. "But my brother does, and that's the only way I can get them to him."

Did you hear that Mrs. Shepherd crossed a sheep with a Brontosaurus?

The animal gave an incredible amount of wool, but every time she used it to knit a sweater, the neck was too long.

Mr. Zumwalt bought his wife a dinosaur for their anniversary. She was a little surprised, but he tried to make her feel better by telling her, "This is a magic dinosaur. Every day she lays a golden egg."

Mrs. Zumwalt didn't really believe this, but as she stared at the dinosaur, it began to grimace and strain, just as if it were laying an egg.

"However," Mr. Zumwalt continued, "there is a down side. You see—"

"Hush, dear, I'm watching," interrupted Mrs. Z. The dinosaur's eyes rolled back in her head, and she gave an awful grunt, and then suddenly she laid a golden egg.

Mrs. Z turned to her husband, but before she could say anything, the dinosaur gave out a tremendous roar, so great that the windows of every house on the block shattered.

"The down side," repeated Mr. Z., "is that we have to live fifty miles outside of town."

"Calvin, can you use the word *bitter* in a sentence?"

"Sure. 'My sister met a dinosaur in the forest and it bitter.' "

"I got a pet Brontoway," bragged Randy.

"What's a Brontoway?" asked Stacey.

"About twenty tons."

"I'm such a compulsive shopper," Lauren confessed. "I'm just like a Tyrannosaurus Rex."

"What do you mean?" asked Megan.

"I charge everything."

117

Wendy went into the butcher store. "Would you give me something for my dinosaur?" she asked.

"Why?" said the butcher. "What would I do with him?"

Did you hear about the midget dentist who treated the Tyrannosaurus with a toothache?

He didn't want to, but someone put him up to it.

"Quick!" came the call to the police station. "There's a Tyrannosaurus terrorizing Elm Street!"

"Did you run away from it?" the lazy police officer asked.

"Of course I did," cried the distraught citizen.

"Then there's no reason for us to come," the officer replied. "That's all we'd do."

The Tyrannosaurus made its way to another town, and began scaring the people there.

A woman called the police. "Hurry, there's a dinosaur eating people outside my house!"

"How do we get there?" the officer asked.

"In a car!"

"Don't tell me you believe your husband when he says he spent the day hunting dinosaurs," sniffed Millicent's mother. "I'll bet he didn't bring a single one home."

"That's why I believe him," said Millicent. "When he goes fishing, he doesn't catch any fish either."

Three cavemen were being chased by a Tyrannosaurus when they came upon a magic lamp. They rubbed it and a genie appeared.

"I will grant you each one wish," the genie said.

"I wish I was back home in my cave with Uga, my wife," said the first caveman.

Poof! He was gone.

"I wish I was back home in my cave, too," said the second.

Poof! He was gone.

By now the Tyrannosaurus was only twenty feet away.

"Gosh," said the third caveman. "I don't know where I should go. I wish those other guys were here to help me decide."

Little Fred wanted a dinosaur for a pet. But his father told him that he couldn't have one unless he learned to behave himself.

Fred tried to be good for a few days, but he still kept getting into trouble.

"Maybe you should pray to Jesus to help you be good," his father suggested.

So Fred went to his room and knelt down to pray. "Jesus," he said. "Pease help me be good."

But the next day, Fred couldn't help himself, and he hit his sister and got into trouble.

So he prayed again, and said, "Jesus, please, please, help me to be good. I really want a dinosaur."

This time Fred only went three hours before he broke a window and was in trouble again.

"Please, Jesus, you have to help me be good. I just have to have a dinosaur," he prayed.

But as soon as he went downstairs, he fell down and swore and his father was very angry.

This time Fred went upstairs and got a statue of the Virgin Mary from his mother's room. He took it to his room and wrapped it in a towel and hid it in a shoe box. Then he knelt down to pray one more time.

"Jesus, if you ever want to see your mother again . . ."

The editors of the *Prehistoric Times* ran an obituary notice for Rex, the fiercest Tyrannosaurus in the jungle. However, it turned out that Rex wasn't really dead. The next day they ran a correction.

It read: "We regret to report that the news of Rex's death was an error."

A few days later Rex attacked a Stegosaurus and wounded it badly. The headline in the *Prehistoric Times* read, "DINOSAUR ATTACKED BY REX IS CRITICAL."

As the Brontosaurus said, "Well, you can hardly blame him."

Gus the Goofasaurus went to his doctor to ask a question. "How long can someone live without a brain?"

"I'm not sure," said the doctor. "How old are you?"

The Smiths were driving along on their vacation when little Timmy said, "My dinosaur has to go wee."

Mr. Smith said, "Your dinosaur is just a stuffed toy. It doesn't have to go wee."

They drove along a little more, and Timmy said, "My dinosaur really has to go wee."

Mr. Smith said, "Timmy, we don't have time to stop. He just has to wait."

A little further down the road Timmy began to cry. "My dinosaur just has to go wee!"

"All right," Mr. Smith grumbled. "There's a gas station just ahead. We'll pull in there."

They turned into the gas station and stopped. "Now you can let your dinosaur go wee," Mr. Smith said.

"Hurray!" cried Timmy. And he picked up his dinosaur and cried, "Whee!"

Lisa and Devon were at the museum. "That dinosaur looks just like Janet," Lisa said.

"You shouldn't say things like that," Devon admonished.

"It's okay. The dinosaur can't hear me."

"I'll give you five dollars if you let me into your basement to play with your Tyrannosaurus," George said.

"Okay," said Dan. "But you have to pay me first."

"No, after," said George.

"First," said Dan. "Because if I let you into the basement to play with my Tyrannosaurus, you aren't going to come back."

"Waitress, why is there a footprint in my dinosaur steak?"

"You said you wanted a dinosaur steak with french fries, and step on it."

HENNY: I don't think our next-door neighbor likes our son.

HANK: Why?

HENNY: Because this afternoon he gave him a knife and asked him if he knew what was inside the dinosaurs at the zoo!

Poor Ms. Stephanopolous was attacked by a rogue Brontosaurus on her trip to Australia. Barely conscious, she was rushed to the hospital, where she lapsed into a coma. When she awoke, she remembered with a shudder what had happened to her, and convinced she was doomed, she asked a nurse, "Was I brought here to die?"

"Oh, no, dearie," the nurse replied. "You've been here a week already."

Cindy was walking home from the library when she met Gary. "What are you reading?" he asked.

"Well," she said. "When I read *Twice Told Tales* my dinosaur laid two eggs. When I read *The Three Musketeers* she laid three eggs. So now I'm reading *Ali Baba and the Forty Thieves!*"

STEVE: My dinosaur is so smart he has brains enough for two.

ALLEN: Then he's the right one for you.

125

One night in the loony bin a patient yelled, "I'm Tyrannosaurus Rex, the king of the dinosaurs!"

"How do you know?" cried another patient.

"Because God told me so," the first one growled.

"I did not!" came the shout from a third cell.

"Send for the veterinarian!" cried Mr. Blaikie. "The dinosaur just swallowed a hundred dollars in quarters!"

"I think we ought to send for a lawyer," said Mrs. Blaikie. "They can get money out of anybody."

A caveman was taking his son out into the jungle to train him to hunt.

"What would you do if a Tyrannosaurus charged at you from the north?" he asked.

"I'd throw my spear at it," his son replied.

"And if another Tyrannosaurus charged at you from the east?"

"I'd throw my spear at it."

"And if one charged at you from the west?"

"I'd throw my spear at it, too."

"Just a second, son," the caveman said. "Where are you getting all these spears?"

"Same place you're getting all these Tyrannosaurus," came the answer.

126

Three Brontosaurus were migrating across a huge glacier. They stopped for the night, and to distract his family from the bitter weather, the father Brontosaurus said, "I've got a tale to tell."

The mother Brontosaurus realized what he was up to, and she said, "I've also got a tale to tell."

Their little baby Brontosaurus piped up, "My tale is told."

MONA: Did you know that every dinosaur had three tails?

LAURA: They did not.

MONA: I'll prove it. Any dinosaur has more tail than no dinosaur, right? And no dinosaur had two tails, right? So every dinosaur must have had three tails.

FARMER ZUMWALT: Does that Tyrannosaurus you're using for a scarecrow work?

FARMER HALLWORTH: Sure does. The crows are so scared they're bringing back the seeds they stole last month.

MARY: Who went into the lion's den and came out alive?

PETER: Daniel.

MARY: And who went into the Tyrannosaurus's den and came out alive?

PETER: Beats me.

MARY: The Tyrannosaurus.

Amy went into the jewelry store and saw a Dryosaurus hanging from the ceiling. "What's he doing up there?" she asked the jeweler.

"He's harmless," the man told her. "He thinks he's a lightbulb."

"Can't you get him to come down?"

"What? And work in the dark?"

KARL: How do you spell "Rontosaurus?"

MAX: Don't you mean "Brontosaurus?"

KARL: No, I figured out the "B" already.

ALLAN: Where's your dinosaur from?

SHIRLEY: California.

ALLAN: What part?

SHIRLEY: All of him.

MABEL: My dinosaur lays square eggs.

HAZEL: That's amazing.

MABEL: And she talks, too.

HAZEL: What does she say?

MABEL: "Ouch."

A Diplodocus, a Stegosaurus, and a Goof-asaurus went to a costume party. The Diplodocus was wearing pointy ears. "I'm Spock," he said. The Stegosaurus was wearing black pants, black boots, and a red shirt. "I'm Scotty," he announced. The Goofasaurus was dressed as a tree. He told the others, "I'm the captain's log."

"My mom told my dad to go to the store to buy some ground beef for hamburgers. But on the way he was attacked by a Tyrannosaurus."

"Heavens! What did your mom do?"

"She made tuna casserole."

The remote village was being terrorized by a ferocious Tyrannosaurus. Every evening it would carry another person off. Word of their plight came to O'Malley, the famous dinosaur hunter, and he agreed to come and save the village.

His first night there, O'Malley set himself up near where the Tyrannosaurus had last struck. Very soon he heard a tremendous crashing, and he knew the Tyrannosaurus was getting near. A minute went by, and he saw two great red eyes glowing in the dark. The space between them was so big that O'Malley knew this had to be the largest Tyrannosaurus that had ever existed.

He took out his rifle and fired.

Nothing happened. Still the eyes got closer.

He fired again.

Nothing happened. The eyes were almost upon him.

Terrified, he switched on a flashlight . . .

. . . and saw *two* Tyrannosaurs, each with one eye closed.

"Did you actually see my client's Tyrannosaurus bite off Mr. Jones's hand?"

"No, but I saw him swallow it."

ANN: If you were in the jungle and a Tyrannosaurus charged you, what would you do?

ROBBY: Pay him.

ROBBY: Please tell me the story about the green Ultrasaurus.

ANN: No. I don't tell off-color stories.

DAD: Please take the dinosaur out and give him some air.

DORA: Okay. Where's the nearest gas station?

DORA: Look at the bunch of dinosaurs.

HAYLEY: Not bunch, herd.

DORA: Heard what?

HAYLEY: Herd of dinosaurs.

DORA: Sure I've heard of dinosaurs.

HAYLEY: No, I mean a dinosaur herd.

DORA: I don't care. I'm not afraid of them.

GOOFASAURUS: My stomach has been hurting ever since I ate those oysters.

VETERINARIAN: Were they fresh?

GOOFASAURUS: How can you tell?

VET: What did they look like when you opened their shells?

GOOFASAURUS: You're supposed to open the shells?

The famous explorer was giving a lecture about his adventures. The climax of his speech came when he told of coming upon the fossilized remains of two Tyrannosaurus locked in mortal combat.

"I remember that discovery as if it were yesterday. There are some spectacles that one never forgets," he announced.

"Gee," said Mr. Fuddy from the back row. "Can you get me a pair? I'm always losing mine."

"I don't know what's wrong with this match," said Gus the Goofasaurus.

"Won't it light?" asked Sally the Smartasaurus.

"It did this morning!"

"I don't understand something else," said Gus.

"What?" said Sally.

"Well, I walked three miles today, and I only moved four feet."

"And another thing," Gus complained. "I keep having these dreams where I'm trying to go through a door with a big sign on it. I push and I push, and it won't open."

"What does the sign say?" sighed Sally.

"Pull."

"Even worse," Gus went on. "I can't get this jar of peanut butter open, even though I'm dancing as hard as I can."

"Why on earth are you dancing?" Sally wondered.

"It says right on the lid, 'twist to open.' "

Seventeen female sheep were arrested last week. They were being herded down Main Street when a Tyrannosaurus started chasing them and they turned tail and ran the other way.

What was the charge?

They made a ewe turn.

The Tyrannosaurus was on a rampage across Texas. He came to the Flagler ranch and ate seven of their prize bulls. He was so proud of himself that he let out a huge roar.

But Six-Guns Flagler, the meanest shot in the West, heard him. She came riding after the Tyrannosaurus on her big white horse. The dinosaur tried to escape, but it was so full that it couldn't run very fast.

Six-Guns Flagler caught up with him in no time and killed him with a single shot, saving thousands of lives.

The moral: When you're full of bull, keep your mouth shut.

SANDRA: Do you know where the telegraph office is? I've got to wire my dinosaur.

AMY: Why? Can't he stand up by himself?

Three paleontologists were on a dig for dinosaur fossils. They had to be very careful so as not to disturb a nearby burial ground for Pueblo Indians.

They worked and worked for months, and finally they came across some bones. The bones seemed a little small for a dinosaur, but they eagerly sent them off to the lab at the university for analysis.

The report came back: "You idiots, these are not two hundred million-year-old dinosaur bones. They are the hundred-year-old bones of a common horse. Come back at once. You have disturbed the burying place of an important Pueblo chief, who was laid to rest with his favorite horse."

"We're ruined," cried the first paleontologist. "Our careers are over!"

"I don't see why," said the second.

"Because," said the third, "no one takes you seriously after you make this kind of grave mistake."

MARK: Where are you going with that gun?

NORMAN: I'm hunting dinosaurs.

MARK: There aren't any dinosaurs around here.

NORMAN: I know that. If there were, I wouldn't have to hunt for them.

NORMAN: Well, you don't need a gun anyway. I've been dinosaur hunting with nothing but a club.

MARK: Wasn't that dangerous?

NORMAN: Not really. We have a hundred members in our club.

A dinosaur wanted to play for the New York Yankees. He pleaded with George Steinbrenner, but Steinbrenner kept telling him no. "Who ever heard of a dinosaur hitting a baseball?" he laughed.

The dinosaur persuaded Steinbrenner to come down to the stadium. One of the players pitched a ball, the dinosaur swung, and the ball sailed clear out of Yankee Stadium.

"You're hired," Steinbrenner said.

Two days later, it was the dinosaur's first turn at bat. He swung, connected, and sent the ball right out of the park. Then he just stood there.

"Run! Run, you stupid lizard!" Steinbrenner shouted from his box.

The dinosaur just looked at him and said, "Who ever heard of a dinosaur running bases?"

Two Tyrannosaurus jumped onto a train as it was heading up a mountain. They burst into the freight car, which was full of chickens. The first one grabbed a chicken and stuffed the whole thing into his mouth.

Just then the train entered a tunnel.

"Hey," said the first Tyrannosaurus. "Have you eaten one of those chickens yet?"

"No," said the second.

"Well, don't. I ate just one and went blind."

Recipe for Dinosaur Soup:

  2 large dinosaurs
  2 cases of onions, chopped
  2 rabbits

Cut the dinosaurs into small, bite-size pieces. Coat them with flour, and fry in butter with the onions until brown. Add water and simmer for a month. Serves 5,000.

If you need to feed more people, you can add the rabbits. But be aware that most people don't like hare in their soup.

Gus went to a fortune teller to find out his fate.

"I will answer any two questions you ask for one thousand dollars," said the fortune teller.

"Don't you think a thousand dollars is a lot to ask for just two questions?" said Gus.

"No, it isn't," said the fortune teller. "Now, what is your second question?"

ANN: What's the difference between an orange, a dinosaur, and a brick?

ROBBY: I give up.

ANN: You can squeeze an orange, but you can't squeeze a dinosaur.

ROBBY: What about the brick?

ANN: I just threw that in to make it hard.

How many Goofasaurus does it take to screw in a light bulb?

Eleven. One to hold the bulb and ten to turn the house.

Mr. Fuddy was driving across country with a truckload of dinosaurs. He pulled into a gas station, and while he was filling his tank, a man walked over.

"Say there, buddy," he exclaimed. "What you got in the truck?"

"Dinosaurs," Mr. Fuddy replied.

"Dinosaurs! Why, my little boy would be tickled pink if I brought him home one of those things. Tell you what, I'm a gambler by nature. If I can guess how many dinosaurs you have in that truck, you give me one."

"Heck," said Mr. Fuddy. "I don't think you can. In fact, if you guess right, I'll give you them *both*."

A Tyrannosaurus was prowling the jungle when she came upon two men sitting under a tree. One was reading a book, while the other was typing away on a portable computer.

Why did the Tyrannosaurus eat the man with a book and let the one with the computer get away?

Because everyone knows that readers digest but writers cramp.

The brave caveman Leif went off on a dangerous dinosaur hunt. He was gone for years and years, and when he finally returned to his village, he found out that he was no longer considered to live there.

He started yelling at the chief, who cringed and said, "I'm sorry, I don't know what happened. I guess we just took Leif off our census."

At two o'clock in the morning, Mike's phone rang. He struggled out of bed to answer it. "This is your next door neighbor," the voice shouted. "I'm just calling to let you know that your pet Stegosaurus is making enough racket to wake the whole block up."

And the caller hung up.

The next night, Mike set his alarm for two A.M., and when he awoke he called his neighbor. He said, "I'm just calling to let you know that I don't have a pet Stegosaurus."

"Grampa," asked Millie. "Was it true that you used to train dinosaurs when you were younger?"

"It sure was, Millie. I got started on my career when I was shipwrecked in the South Pacific near an island called Fradge. It was covered with dinosaurs, and pretty soon I taught a few of them tricks. I was rescued by a freighter ship, and when I left I brought some of the critters along with me. I spent about five years touring the country before I met your grandmother and decided to settle down."

"What did you do with the dinosaurs?"

"Oh, I put 'em in a great big crate. And on the side I wrote 'Fradge Isle, Handle with Care.'"

ROBBY: What did the dinosaur say when his mind went blank?

ANN: I can't imagine.

ROBBY: That's right!

CHARLIE: When I was your age, I was chased by a Tyrannosaurus.

DORA: That must have been the worst thing that ever happened to you.

CHARLIE: No, that was when he caught me.

"Will you marry me?" Mr. Fuddy asked Amanda.

"I'm not sure. I talked to both the other women you were married to, and they told me all about how you keep dinosaurs in the basement."

"Oh, don't pay them any attention," Mr. Fuddy assured her. "Those are just old wives' tales."

"I had a nightmare about being chased by a Tyrannosaurus. It seemed like I'd never get away."

"Did you?"

"Not in my wildest screams."

A dino from Kalamazoo
Dreamt he was eating a shoe.
He awoke with a fright
In the middle of the night.
Now instead of one tongue, he has two.

A Tyrannosaurus was rampaging across a golf course and came upon a lone golfer. He promptly ate the fellow.

At least the man died happy. He had a fairway look in his eyes.

The two Carnosaurus hated eating chicken, but there was almost nothing else nearby. Pretty soon they had eaten every animal but the chickens. One turned to the other and said, "It's no use, we'll just have to bite the pullet."

Gus went to see a psychic because he was having terrible dreams about being eaten by a Tyrannosaurus. "Tell me," he said, "am I going to die?"

"Die?" said the psychic. "That's the last thing you're going to do."

Did you hear that Gus went to a poker game? The other dinosaurs wouldn't let him play, so he watched and imagined that he was being dealt a hand. He kept losing, and pretty soon he lost his mind.

The site of a huge dinosaur fossil dig was rumored to be haunted. The reporter from the news magazine went there with a camera and waited up all night. Sure enough, about three in the morning, the ghosts of all kinds of dinosaurs began to appear.

As the reporter grabbed his camera and began snapping pictures, the ghosts seemed to notice. They paraded past him, one after another, each one seeming to want to have its picture taken.

The next day, the reporter rushed to have the pictures developed, thinking he would soon be famous. However, all that he got were a bunch of dark smudges. As he told his editor, "The spirits were willing, but the flash was weak."

Once Upon a Snaurus

How do you bathe a dinosaur?
First you get a very large tub . . .

Where do you buy shoes for a Yangchuanosaurus?
In a shoe store!

Where do French dinosaurs come from?
France!

Why do dinosaurs choose to play the tim-
pani in an orchestra?
Because they have trouble holding a bow!

Why was the dinosaur begging for money
on the street corner?
He needed money for the subway home!

How can you tell if there's a dinosaur in
your refrigerator?
Open the door!

146

Can you name the famous dare-devil dinosaur?
Evel Knievelsaurus!

How do dinosaurs celebrate birthdays?
With a party and lots of people crackers!

Why is it important to support dinosaur public television?
Dinosaurs may be extinct, but they mustn't be forgotten!

Where do Hypacrosaurus buy their camping equipment?
At L. L. Dinobean!

How many dinosaurs does it take to fix a flat tire?
Two. One to pick up the car and one to change the tire!

Can you name the famous dinosaur toy store?
F. A. O. Schwarzosaurus!

Why do dinosaurs avoid junk food?
It raises their cholesterol level!

Why do dinosaurs use umbrellas?
To stay dry!

Name two favorite dinosaur television programs.
Northern Dino.
Barney.

What do dinosaurs call small dogs?
Puppies.

What did the Triceratops take to prevent sea sickness?
Dinomine!

What do you get when you cross a Brontosaurus with a monkey?
A dinosaur with a curly tail!

What happens when you tease a dinosaur?
Who knows? There are no survivors to tell us!

What happens when two dinosaurs fall in love?
They usually get married and have baby dinosaurs!

What is so special about a Lapparentosaurus?
Nothing. It's just another dinosaur!

What did the Brontosaurus say after the Ceratosaurus bit off her tail?
"Ouch!"

Why do Carnosaurus generally suffer from bad health?
They don't eat vegetables!

How do mother and father dinosaurs punish their children?
Carefully!

What kind of dinosaurs are famous for moonshine?
Dystylosaurus!

Can you name the famous dinosaur family from Virginia that moved to California?
The Beverly Dinobillies!

Why are Psittacosaurus always depressed?
They don't get enough attention in dinosaur studies!

Why are Archosaurus, Agrosaurus, Apatosaurus, and Allosaurus best buddies?
They can all share their initial sweaters!

Where do Albisaurus do their laundry?
At the dinomat!

Why do dinosaurs prefer motorcycles instead of cars?
More head and tail room!

Where do Troodons live?
With their families!

What do you give a Barosaurus with a cough?
A megadose of tea with honey and a lot of room!

What did the Teratosaurus have after the school baseball game?
A saur throat!

Have you heard about the famous American Indian dinosaur?
Geronimo Rex!

What's the most popular job at Jurassic Village?
Dinosaur trainer!

What do you get when you cross a Stegasaurus with a diamond?
An expensive, glittering dinosaur!

What is the most popular car in dinosaur-land?
The Taurus!

Where do Diplodocus buy their jeans?
At Dino-Gap!

What do dinosaurs like to have with their milk?
Dog biscuits!

"Did you hear about the dinosaur that went exploring in the Grand Canyon?"
"No. What happened?"
"He found many lost relatives!"

What was the most popular prehistoric novel?
Gone with the Dinowind!

What do you do if a dinosaur steals your parking space?
Look for another one!

What is the prognosis for a dinosaur that swallows a stick of dynamite?
He will never suffer from constipation!

What is the best way to contact a Ceratosaurus traveling in Europe?
A dino-gram!

What do you call a dinosaur that runs faster than light?
A speed-dino!

What do you call a Sauropod judge?
Your Honorsaurus!

Where did the Pteradon keep his identification?
In his pocket!

CHILD ONE: "My grandparents gave me a dinosaur for my birthday, but it didn't have any ears. What do you think I should call it?"
CHILD TWO: "Nothing. It won't hear you anyway!"

DINOSAUR ONE: "I'm going on my first date tonight. I'm curious about how long female dinosaurs should be kissed?"
DINOSAUR TWO: "The same time as short female dinosaurs!"

DINOSAUR ONE: "I've been having trouble sleeping for months now. Do you think it's serious?"
DINOSAUR TWO: "To tell you the truth, I wouldn't lose any sleep over it!"

DINOSAUR ONE: "I have been taking thousands of pictures; do you think they're any good?"
DINOSAUR TWO: "I'll reserve comment. I don't want to make any snap decisions!"

If you have a dinosaur stuck in your bathtub, what should you do?
Pull the plug!

What do you call a dinosaur that steals things without realizing it?
A Kleptosaurus!

What's going to happen to the dinosaur that only eats yeast and furniture polish?
I imagine that he will rise and shine regularly!

DINOSAUR: "I'm losing my memory. What should I do?"
DOCTOR DINOSAUR: "Try to forget the problem!"

DINOSAUR ONE: "I'm too skinny. What can I do?"
DINOSAUR TWO: "The best way to get fat is from the butcher."

DINOSAUR ONE: "I inherited a peanut farm. Is it healthy to eat them or are they fattening?"
DINOSAUR TWO: "Of course they're fattening. Have you ever seen a skinny elephant?"

Why do dinosaurs prefer to drive garbage trucks?
They like things at their disposal!

Why do dinosaurs like to go scuba diving?
They like to study things in depth!

How do dinosaur sailors clean their clothes?
They throw them overboard to be washed ashore!

Do dinosaurs look good in tight jeans?
Not the bulk of them!

DINOSAUR ONE: "Should I get a kitten for my brother?"
DINOSAUR TWO: "It sounds like a fair trade to me!"

Why do dinosaurs take a lot of baths?
Because grime doesn't pay!

How do Brontosaurus on submarine duty communicate?
In Dino-code!

What do you call dinosaurs that make sculptures out of 7-UP bottles?
Pop artists!

DINOSAUR ONE: "What is the definition of ignorance?"
DINOSAUR TWO: "I don't know!"

Why do dinosaurs avoid studying astronomy?
It's over their heads!

How can you keep a dinosaur from smelling?
Hold its nose!

What kind of cars do Swedish dinosaurs like to rent?
Fjords!

DINOSAUR ONE: "I'm taking a trip to New Zealand. Should I take a ship?"
DINOSAUR TWO: "A suitcase would be more useful!"

How do you keep a dinosaur from charging?
Take away its credit cards!

Why don't dinosaurs like to work in bowling alleys?
Because they can only earn pin money!

Why don't dinosaurs last as professional coffee makers?
They can't stand the daily grind!

What do you call a dinosaur that keeps to himself and avoids contact with people?
A Reclusasaurus!

How do dinosaurs avoid wrinkles?
They don't sleep in their clothes!

Have you heard about the Brontosaurus that is always butting into other dinosaurs' business?
He suffers from an interferiority complex!

Have you heard about the paleontologist that stole an Egyptian dinosaur?
Tut, tut!

Why don't dinosaurs like to sleep in beds?
Because their tails hang over the edge!

What is the first thing a Teratosaurus learns in school?
The Dino-bet! The alpha-dino!

TEACHER: Name four members of the dinosaur family.
STUDENT: Mother, father, sister, and brother!

Why do dinosaurs like to play with elephants?
They love to tickle those ivories!

Can you name the famous dinosaur novel by Mark Twain?
Huckelsaurus Finn!

DINOSAUR ONE: "I'm glad my name is Ian."
DINOSAUR TWO: "Why?"
DINOSAUR ONE: "Because that's what everyone calls me!"

Dinosaur Prayer:

Now I lay me down to rest
I pray to wake tomorrow with zest
If I should die in battle later
Cancel my breakfast order with the waiter!

What kind of tests do they give dinosaurs?
Dino-aminations!

Roses are red
Violets are blue
Dinosaurs are old
And you are too!

NORMAN: "May I bring my pet dinosaur to school?"
TEACHER: "No!"

Where do blue Ultrasaurus eggs come from?
From sad Ultrasaurus!

TEACHER: "Haley, spell dinosaur."
HALEY: "D-I-N-O-S-A-U"
TEACHER: "OK, but what's on the end?"
HALEY: "I think a tail!"

What would happen to you if a Psittacosaurus sat in front of you in class?
You probably couldn't see the blackboard!

DINOSAUR ONE: "I'm teacher's pet."
DINOSAUR TWO: "How come?"
DINOSAUR ONE: "She couldn't afford a
horse!"

Where do dinosaurs sleep?
On mattrapods!

BOB: In this box I have a ten-foot dinosaur.
ORIN: Don't be ridiculous. Everyone knows
that dinosaurs only have two feet!

How do you stop a dinosaur polio epi-
demic?
With a dino-accination!

Why don't dinosaurs use the yellow pages?
Because their fingers are tired!

How do you begin a story about a dinosaur?
Once upon a snaurus . . .

What do you call a dinosaur that always puts things off?
A procrastinsaurus!

Why did the dinosaur put a pencil in his ear?
He wanted to be a leader!

Can you name the most famous talk-show host from the Triassic period?
Johnny Carsonaurus!

What do you get when you cross a dinosaur with an orange?
Gallons and gallons of juice!

What do you call a dinosaur from Australia?
An Aussiepod!

What did the Stenosaurus put at the beginning of her book?
A Dino-ication!

What do you call a dinosaur that earns a living by playing cards?
A Sharkosaurus!

What musical key do dinosaurs sing in?
D-ino flat!

Why are dinosaurs natural musicians?
Their tongues are sharp and their heads are flat!

Why did Luciano Dinosaur bring a ladder to his concert?
He wanted to sing higher notes!

Why did the Triceratops bring a vegetable to his piano lesson?
Because the teacher told him that his playing would improve if he had a beet!

Why don't dinosaurs need piano benches?
They just lean on their tails!

What do Crocodilias like to eat with onion dip?
Dinochips!

What do dinosaurs like to drink with pizza?
Cokasaurus!

What kind of food do Sauropod mathematicians eat?
Square meals!

Why do dinosaurs prefer to fly first class?
More tail room!

Where can we find dinosaurs?
We don't have to. Anything that big doesn't get lost!

164

Dinosaurs in the forest,
Fish in the sea,
How you passed English,
Is a mystery to me!

Why are dinosaurs good plumbers?
Because their tails are natural snakes!

Why do dinosaurs get good grades in history?
Because of the thousands of years they don't have to remember!

What do dinosaurs make when they want to get together?
Dates . . .

And what do they talk about on these dates?
The good old days!

Dinosaur history is a subject very dear to me,
Although the topic was once dead as can be,
Everyone is now copying me!

Where do dinosaurs learn to kill dragons?
In night school!

Can you say Yangchuanosaurus five times quickly?
Try again!

What is the most popular dinosaur long-distance telephone company?
Allosaurus, Triceratops, and Teratosaurus! (AT&T)

Ode to a dinosaur:

When he dies, bury him deep,
Bury the history to keep, keep, keep.
Tell the world he's gone to rest,
And won't return without a paleontologist quest!

The more dinosaurs study,
The more they know,
The more they know,
The more there is to forget,
The more there is to forget,
The less they know,
So why should dinosaurs study?

What reference work do dinosaurs use to look up the meaning or spelling of words?
A thesaurus!

What happens to the dinosaur and dog that go to school together?
They graduate at the same time!

Did you hear about the very bad Hypacrosaurus?
He was expelled from obedience school!

What type of bikes do Pterodactyls like to ride?
Dinospeeds!

Do dinosaurs tell time?
No. They need a watch!

Did you hear about the dumb Helopus?
He flunked recess!

What do dinosaurs use when they sky-dive?
A Parasaurus!

What course do dinosaurs excel in?
Prehistory!

What three R's do dinosaurs learn in school?
Run, run, run!

Can you name a famous dinosaur fairy princess?
Cinderallosaurus!

How are dinosaurs and hippopotamuses alike?
Neither can play tennis!

How do dinosaurs on the starship Enterprise shave?
With laser blades!

There was a dinosaur with a brush,
Who painted many pictures in a rush.
To enhance her creations,
She drew illustrations
With a pen instead of a brush!

There was a young dinosaur whose delight
Was to capture birds in flight.
He trapped them in bad weather,
And admired their feathers,
As they tried to fly out of sight!

Dinosaur tips:

Be careful not to catch your tail in taxi
doors!
Be sure to floss your teeth every day!
Be sure to wear sneakers with good
arches for support while running!
Use body lotion for all the dry scales!

There was a dinosaur from Key West,
Whose sand castles were the best.
Every time he built it,
A wave would tilt it,
A problem for the dinosaur from Key West.

There was a dinosaur who enjoyed skating
on the lake,
Though he did sometimes make a mistake.
Because he was small and not very tall,
The best he could do was fall!

There was a dinosaur from Van Nuys,
Who was very fond of blueberry pies.
His friends would tease him,
And that wouldn't please him,
But he still had his pies.

There was a dinosaur from Niagara Falls,
He loved to play with basketballs.
While in search of new playmates,
He lost his regular teammates,
The dinosaur from Niagara Falls.

There was a lost dinosaur with sore feet,
Who had very little to eat.
He was looking for a home,
And he roamed and roamed,
And one day he was rescued from the
street!

There was a baby dinosaur from San Diego,
Who didn't know where other dinosaurs go.
He went to the zoo,
But couldn't find anybody he knew,
Poor little dinosaur from San Diego.

There was a Brontosaurus from Goshen,
Who always loved lots of commotion.
From time to time she would rest,
To control her endless zest.
But there was no controlling her emotion.

There was a dinosaur from Duluth,
Whose manners were uncouth.
He slurped from his cup,
And dropped shells from nuts,
This rude dinosaur from Duluth.

There was a dinosaur in bed,
Who slept with a nightcap on his head.
With the sunrise,
Came open eyes,
For this dinosaur in bed.

There was a dinosaur from Montclair,
Who liked to float through the air.
The problem at hand,
Was that he was stuck in the sand,
And couldn't leave Montclair by air!

Did you hear about the musical Elasmosaurus?
He stretches to Beethoven every morning!

What kind of dinosaurs were lost at sea?
Titanosaurus!

What is strange about the Pisanosaurus?
It has an uncontrollable attraction for Italy!

What kind of dinosaurs prefer to jog on a track?
Laplatasaurus!

Have you heard about the Late Cretaceous Titanosaurid Sauropods?
NO? You don't watch enough C-Spansaurus!

What kind of dinosaurs are compelled to have five of everything?
Pentaceratops!

The Four-Door
Brontosaur

How did the dinosaur get out of jail?
He scaled the wall.

What did dinosaurs use to cover their
floors?
Rep-tiles.

Why didn't the Tyrannosaurus eat the
green Stegosaurus?
He was waiting for it to ripen.

What would you get if you crossed a Do-
berman pinscher and a Tyrannosaurus?
A very frightened mail carrier.

Did you hear about the two Brontosaurus
that met in a revolving door?
They started going around together.

What did the Carnosaurus say when it met
the Diplodocus?
"Pleased to eat you."

What do you get if you cross an Ultrasaurus with a frankfurter?
The world's biggest hot dog.

Why shouldn't you grab a dinosaur's tail?
It may be the dinosaur's tail, but it could be your end.

Why did the Triceratops try to climb the Empire State Building?
It thought it was King Kong.

Why did the Tyrannosaurus terrorize the village?
It thought it was Frankenstein.

What do you get if you cross a Tyrannosaurus with a cat?
Something that needs an awfully big scratching post.

Why did Billy want to buy a Ferris wheel?
His Allosaurus thought it was a gerbil.

What do you call a dinosaur that walks like a duck and quacks like a duck?
If it walks like a duck and quacks like a duck, it's a duck.

What do you get if you cross a Tyrannosaurus with a beaver?
A monster that chops down Brontosaurus.

What did the Frugal Gourmet do when he met a Stegosaurus?
He made Stegosaurus Tartare.

What do you get if you cross an Ultrasaurus with a Weber grill?
All-you-can-eat barbecue.

Why couldn't the Brontosaurus make a snowsuit?
Because it couldn't find a long enough zipper.

What do you get if you cross a Tyrannosaurus with a computer?
A dinosaur with a mega-bite.

How did the Tyrannosaurus scare itself?
It looked in the mirror.

Why did the Police Department hire a Tyrannosaurus?
The officers wanted to take a bite out of crime.

Why did the Brontosaurus apply for Social Security?
He was 250 million years old.

What did the Ultrasaurus say when it saw Lake Superior?
"Look, a puddle."

What do you get if you cross a Tyrannosaurus with a door-to-door salesman?
I don't know, but buy whatever it's selling.

What do you get if you cross a Tyrannosaurus with marsh grass?
Rex Reed.

What was the name of Superman's dinosaur enemy?
Rex Ruthor.

What did the mother Tyrannosaurus call her six babies?
Rex-tuplets.

Why did the boy Tyrannosaurus like the girl Tyrannosaurus?
She had Rex appeal.

What did the witch use to turn the prince into a Tyrannosaurus?
A Rex hex.

How do the tellers at the Tyrannosaurus Bank let the customers know they're ready?
They call out, "Next Rex."

What do you call an angry Tyrannosaurus?
A vexed Rex.

Did you hear about the dinosaur production of "A Streetcar Named Desire?"
It stars Marlon Brandosaurus.

What do you call an apartment for a dinosaur?
A bronto condo.

Did you hear about the dinosaur in the window at the cathedral?
It's a stained-glass-saurus.

What kind of dinosaur did the Lone Ranger like best?
The Tonto-saurus.

What kind of dinosaur was always weeping?
The Cryceratops.

What kind of dinosaur lived in the desert?
The Dryceratops.

What kind of dinosaur sauteed its food?
The Fryceratops.

What kind of dinosaur did Tyrannosaurus
like to eat with corned beef?
The Ryceratops.

Which dinosaur was orange?
The Carrotdactyl.

Which dinosaur liked crackers?
The Parrotdactyl.

Which dinosaur looked like an ape?
The Hairydactyl.

Which dinosaur officiated at prehistoric
weddings?
The Marrydactyl.

Which dinosaur was always asking questions?
The Querydactyl.

Which dinosaur was very cautious?
The Warydactyl.

Which dinosaur was always panhandling?
The Begosaurus.

Which dinosaur ran the fastest?
The Legosaurus.

Which dinosaur had a wooden leg?
The Pegosaurus.

Which dinosaur made wine?
The Gallosaurus.

What kind of dinosaur do you make candles from?
The Tallosaurus.

What do you get if you give a dinosaur a pogo stick?
Big holes in your driveway.

What do you get if you give a dinosaur finger paints?
A mess.

What does a Tyrannosaurus call a school bus full of kids?
A lunchbox.

Why did the Goofasaurus put twigs in the salmon he caught?
He wanted fish sticks.

What did the Tyrannosaurus call the swimming pool full of people?
Soup.

Why did the Goofasaurus return the necktie he bought?
It was too tight.

Why couldn't the Tyrannosaurus find the composer he was chasing through the jungle?
He was Haydn.

What did the Tyrannosaurus do when the Goofasaurus threw a grenade at him?
He pulled out the pin and threw it back.

How do you catch a unique dinosaur?
Unique up on it.

How do you catch a tame dinosaur?
Same way. Unique up on it.

Why didn't the Goofasaurus have any ice cubes?
The one who knew the recipe died.

Why did the Goofasaurus give out canaries on Halloween?
He thought it was trick or tweet.

How did the Pterodactyl get to the vet?
Flu.

Did you hear about the Tyrannosaurus that liked fish?
He ate worms and then sat by the river with baited breath.

What's the difference between a fly and a dinosaur?
You can't zip a dinosaur.

Did you hear about the Tyrannosaurus that had a fight with a porcupine?
The porcupine won, on points.

Which opera did the Carnosaurus sing after it caught its dinner?
Aida.

What did the Tyrannosaurus want to do when it grew up?
It was thinking about a career in claw enforcement.

What do you call a Stegosaurus that had a fight with a Tyrannosaurus?
Claude.

Why did the Brontosaurus paint himself pink with a green stripe around the middle?
He thought he was an Easter egg.

When is a dinosaur like a teenager?
When it's between a man and a boy.

What did the Tyrannosaurus do during the blackout?
They turned on each other.

Why wasn't the Pterodactyl hurt when it fell out of the fifty-foot tree?
It was on a branch a foot off the ground.

What did the superstitious Tyrannosaurus do when a black cat crossed his path?
He ate it.

When is a dinosaur like a teapot?
When you're teasin' it.

Why did the Dalmationasaurus have such
a hard time hiding from Tyrannosaurus?
Because they were always spotted.

What's the difference between a homeless
Tyrannosaurus and a dead bee?
One's a seedy beast, the other's a bee de-
ceased.

What's the difference between buying a
well-trained pet dinosaur and one that
isn't?
One is housebroken; the other leaves your
house broken.

What happened to the Ultrasaurus that
swallowed a cloud of fireflies?
It was filled with delight.

What would you call a Triceratops being
chased by dogs?
Hounded.

How come the Tyrannosaurus ate the Diplodocus three times in a row?
He got the hiccups.

Why did Greg get in trouble for feeding his little sister?
He was trying to feed her to the dinosaurs at the zoo.

What's as big as a Tyrannosaurus, but weighs nothing?
Its appetite.

How many dinosaurs had one leg?
All of them.

What's the hardest part about taming a Tyrannosaurus?
Its teeth.

What do you call a grass-eating dinosaur that likes to be by itself?
The Lone Grazer.

What's big and eats brownies?
A Tyrannosaurus at a Girl Scout camp.

Why is Father Paleo so fondly remembered?
He was the first missionary to give Tyrannosaurus a taste of Christianity.

Why did the Tyrannosaurus want to eat at North's Chuck Wagon?
Because they had a sign out front that said "Children half price."

Why did the aging dinosaur have an AM-FM pacemaker installed?
Because he wanted to have a song in his heart.

What happened to the Goofasaurus that fell into a vat of ginger ale?
Nothing. It was a soft drink.

What do old bread and the back end of a dinosaur have in common?
With bread, you see it's stale; with the back end of a dinosaur, you see its tale.

What happened to the Tyrannosaurus that
ate too much?
It became gnawseated.

What do you get when you cross a Brontosaurus with a pig?
A dinosaur that hogs the swimming pool.

What do you get when you cross a dinosaur
with a dinosaur?
A double-cross.

What time is it when half a dozen Tyrannosaurus are chasing a single Triceratops?
Six after one.

Why did the Tyrannosaurus eat rabbits?
He wanted to improve his eyesight.

What did the Tyrannosaurus do when he
spotted a pig?
He went after it whole hog.

Did you hear about the Tyrannosaurus that gave up eating at Kentucky Fried? He chickened out.

What would get if you crossed an Ultrasaurus with a skunk? A big stink.

Which dinosaurs had four legs and flies? The dead ones.

What would you get if you crossed a Hopasaurus with a constrictor? A bouncing baby boa.

What's a Tyrannosaurus's favorite holiday? Fangsgiving.

Why did Leroy call his Dryosaurus Frank when it was roaming loose, and Ernie when it was caged? Ernie was its pen name.

Which is easier to spell: *bees* or *Diplodocus*? *Bees*. It's spelled with more *e*'s.

"Did you hear about the Stegosaurus that thought he was a vampire?"

"No!"

"It's okay. He went to Dr. Freud and was cured."

"How does he feel now?"

"Not bat."

Did you hear about the Tyrannosaurus that hides in an oasis, masquerading as a dromedary?

His victims don't notice him because he's using camelflage.

Why did the dinosaur cross the road?

To prove it wasn't chicken.

Why couldn't the dinosaur break into the store full of smoked salmon?

It was full of lox.

What do you get if you cross a Brontosaurus with Michael Jordan?

A basketball player that needs four size-16 shoes.

Why did the Brontosaurus want to buy a scarf at Meineke?

Because it heard it "wouldn't pay a lot for a muffler."

What did Brontosaurus like to do on dates?
Neck.

Why shouldn't you give a Stegosaurus china?
Because it already has its own plates.

What do you get if you cross a car with a Triceratops?
An auto with three horns.

What should you do if you see an Ultrasaurus on roller skates?
Get out of the way!

What do you get if you cross a shark with a Tyrannosaurus?
A lawyer.

What should you do if a Brontosaurus eats a lemon?
Pucker up.

What happened to the dinosaur who stuck his feet in a pool of molten metal?
He became a Bronze-toe-saurus.

What's a Tyrannosaurus's favorite school?
Eton.

Did you hear about the Tyrannosaurus prophet?
He was called Gnaws-trodamus.

What do you call a fellow dining on Bronto-steaks?
A man eating dinosaur.

What do you call it when a mouse hits a Brontosaurus?
A low blow.

What do Tyrannosaurus use for toothpicks?
Skinny people.

How come the Ultrasaurus couldn't go on a cruise, but the elephant could?
Because only the elephant had a trunk.

What do you get if you cross an elephant with a dinosaur?
Something that never forgets that it's extinct.

What happened to the Tyrannosaurus that ate the nuclear-power plant?
It came down with atomic ache.

Why did the hungry Tyrannosaurus want to join the Marines?
He heard that they had a few good men.

Why did the rich Brontosaurus buy the QE2?
He wanted to go water skiing.

Why did the Tyrannosaurus steal food?
He wanted a hot meal.

Did you hear about the Tyrannosaurus who was so tough that he ate his meat raw and then sat in a fire to barbecue it?

Why did the Tyrannosaurus eat his masseur?
Because he rubbed him the wrong way.

Did you hear what happened when Gus the Goofasaurus saw a man wearing a sign that said "Free Big Mac?"
He asked the guy, "What did Big Mac do?"

Why didn't the Tyrannosaurus listen to her conscience?
She didn't like to take advice from a stranger.

What's the difference between a songwriter and a dead dinosaur?
One composes, the other decomposes.

Why did the Tyrannosaurus lose the game of pin-the-tail-on-the-donkey?
He ate the tail.

Why was the Brontosaurus arrested for indecent exposure?
He was a nudist.

Do you know why Gus the Goofasaurus failed every class except home economics?
He didn't take home economics.

What did the Dryosaurus say to the mosquito?
"Stop bugging me."

What do you get if you cross a Tyrannosaurus with a chicken?
An alarmed cluck.

What else might you get if you crossed a chicken with a Tyrannosaurus?
Tyrannosaurus Pecks.

What kind of jokes does a Smartosaurus make?
Wisecracks.

What did the dinosaur say to the elevator?
"Can you give me a lift?"

What happened when the Triceratops ate
the muffler?
It was exhausted.

What's worse than seeing a Tyrannosaurus's teeth?
Seeing its tonsils.

What did the funny dinosaur eat for
breakfast?
Cream of wit.

What were the New York Yankees called
during the Jurassic period?
The Bronto Bombers.

What did they call the selfish young Oviraptor?
Mimi.

Which dinosaur invented spaghetti?
The one who used her noodle.

Where did the Syntarsus get a flat tire?
At the fork in the road.

For Sale: Tame Tyrannosaurus. Eats anything. Fond of people.

Why did Gus the Goofasaurus waste his time learning to play the guitar?
It took him a year to figure out that you don't blow into it.

How far did Gus get when he tried to cross the lake in a leaky boat?
About halfway.

What happened to the Tyrannosaurus that ate a window?
He got a pane in his stomach.

What do you get if you cross a banjo with a Bronto?
A dinosaur with a lot of pluck.

Did you know that Tyrannosaurus all hunted bear?
Sure. None of them wore clothes.

What would you get if you crossed a blender with an Ultrasaurus?
A big mix-up.

What do you call a dinosaur that eats hot dogs?
Frank.

How many dinosaurs can you put in an empty cage at the zoo?
Just one. After that it isn't empty.

Why didn't the dinosaur who was lost in the desert starve?
She ate the sand-which is there.

How do you keep a dinosaur from sleep-walking?
Put tacks on the ground.

Why did the dinosaur cross the road?
He was stapled to the punk rocker.

Why did the Tyrannosaurus want to eat in Tinseltown?
He heard there were twenty thousand people in the Hollywood Bowl.

Did Gus the Goofasaurus have a hard time learning to be a garbage collector?
No. He picked it up as he went along.

What kind of dinosaur stands in the corner?
A naughty one.

Did you hear about the paleontologist who was obsessed with studying the Diplodocus?
He was a Diplo-maniac.

What would you get if you crossed a Betasuchus with a rhinoceros?
A Dinoceros.

What would you get if you crossed an Iguanadon with Cyrano de Bergerac?
A Di-nose-saur.

What do you call the creatures that lived in Alaska during the Jurassic period?
Di-Nome-saurs.

What would you call a Stegosaurus that lived forever?
A no-die-saur.

What's the difference between a blind man and a dinosaur that gets seasick?
One can't see to go; the other can't go to sea.

What did one dinosaur say to the other on December 31?
"It's New Year's Eve."

Did you hear about the Triceratops who always wanted to go to Rio de Janiero? He was a Brazil nut.

Why did Gus the Goofasaurus ask for size–twenty-seven bananas? He wanted to make slippers.

If sixteen Tyrannosaurus share one Stegosaurus, what time is it? A quarter to four.

Why did Gus the Goofasaurus put glue on his Tylenol? He had a splitting headache.

Why did Gus mix gunpowder and egg whites? He wanted to make a boom-meringue.

What do you call a Tyrannosaurus in a tent with a sheik's wives? A harem scarem.

What would a dinosaur be if it had a foot on each side and a foot in the middle?
A yardstick.

What kind of dinosaur can't make up its mind about taking a trip?
A stay-go-saurus.

Why did Gus the Goofasaurus eat magnets?
He wanted to be attractive.

Why did the sick dinosaur look pale?
He nearly kicked the bucket.

Why couldn't the Tyrannosaurus get a dress to match her eyes?
They don't make bloodshot dresses.

What's big, lives in swamps, has a long neck, and goes "slam, slam, slam, slam?"
A four-door Brontosaurus.

What was the name of the dinosaur who invented baseball?
Homer.

Why wouldn't Gus the Goofasaurus take any onions on his boat trip?
He didn't want to find out that one was a leek.

What did they call the Tyrannosaurus that liked to chase rabbits?
Bugs Bunny.

What's the best way to take a Brontosaurus's temperature?
With a verrrrrrrrrrrrry long thermometer.

What did they call the dinosaur who kept an encyclopedia in his back pocket?
Smarty pants.

How did the Tyrannosaurus feel after he ate the battery?
He was shocked.

How did the Triceratops feel when he had sore throat and fleas?
Hoarse and buggy.

How did the Tyrannosaurus make a moth-ball?
He stepped on it.

How did Gus the Goofasaurus swim a hundred meters in three seconds?
He went over a waterfall.

Why did the Stegosaurus cross the road?
To get a hamburger. Get it?
Neither did the Stegosaurus.

What's the difference between a butcher and a Triceratops with insomnia?
One weighs a steak, the other stays awake.

How did Gus the Goofasaurus make the piano laugh?
He tickled the ivories.

What was left of the cow after the Tyrannosaurus ate its legs?
Ground beef.

What kind of galoshes did a Stegosaurus
wear on rainy days?
Wet ones.

What did they call the Pterodactyl who
thought she was a jet?
Plane crazy.

CAROL: I can lift a dinosaur with one hand.
RACHEL: I don't believe you.
CAROL: Just show me a dinosaur with one
hand, and I'll lift it.

Why wasn't Rosemary afraid when she
saw the man-eating Tyrannosaurus?
Because she is a woman.

What did the Tyrannosaurus say when it
saw the Metroliner full of people?
"Look, a chew-chew train."

Why did the Tyrannosaurus eat the bottle of shampoo?
It was labelled "Head and Shoulders."

What do you get if you cross a Boy Scout and a Tyrannosaurus?
Something that helps old ladies across the street, then eats them.

Why did Gus the Goofasaurus step on a candy bar?
He wanted to set foot on Mars.

TEACHER: Maxine, why are the dinosaurs extinct?
MAXINE: I don't know, but you can't blame it on me.

Why couldn't Gus the Goofasaurus find the English Channel?
He didn't have a television.

Where does a Tyrannosaurus sit in a
movie theater?
Wherever he wants!

If you want even **MORE**
dinosaur jokes, head to your
local bookstore and look for

1,001 DINOSAUR
JOKES FOR KIDS

by
Alice Saurus

Published by Ballantine Books.

Knock-knock.
Who's there?
Summer.
Summer who?
Summer loony, some are silly, but all of
these jokes are guaranteed fun!
Published by Ballantine Books.